MW01676095

PROSTATE CANCER

No Big Deal: Turned Over to God

BRUCE E. MARSEE

WITH FOREWORD BY
ROBERT BADALAMENT, MD, FACS

PublishAmerica
Baltimore

© 2013 by Bruce E. Marsee.
All rights reserved. No part of this book may be reproduced, stored in a retrieval system or transmitted in any form or by any means without the prior written permission of the publishers, except by a reviewer who may quote brief passages in a review to be printed in a newspaper, magazine or journal.

First printing

PublishAmerica has allowed this work to remain exactly as the author intended, verbatim, without editorial input.

Author photo on back cover produced by Robyn Marsee.

Softcover 9781627096935
PUBLISHED BY PUBLISHAMERICA, LLLP
www.publishamerica.com
Baltimore

Printed in the United States of America

It has been said "The long arm of the pen reaches beyond the grave," because when a man writes, he continues to speak even after his vocal chords expire.

***F**or*

Our sons Kevin and Kerry.

Any Mother or Father would

be proud to say, “These are our sons”.

ACKNOWLEDGMENT

During late 1998 and early 1999 when I had my encounter with Prostate Cancer, (PC) I did a series of articles for a local newspaper related to what I was experiencing with this dreaded male disease. Since then I have spoken with many individuals including relatives, friends and others who also had an encounter with PC. For treatment some selected Radiation, others a Radical Prostatectomy and some Cryosurgery. One did nothing. And some did not make it and passed away. I, on the other hand, left it in God's hands. I experienced no problems whatsoever while others did. For the past ten years, on each annual checkup, my PSA continues to be less than zero. In other words, too low to even matter. During this experience I have learned that most Prostate Cancers are curable if caught in time, but not if one waits too late. As referenced in WorldPress—***Prostate cancer is not the most aggressive form of cancer, to effect men; however, a diagnosis is still serious. A radical prostatectomy is a very invasive form of surgery as the prostate is buried deep within the abdomen.***

While I have been working on a manuscript for a spiritual novel, a couple of close friends and especially my wife Sharon encouraged me to update my PC articles and incorporate them into book form.

It was Sharon's opinion that if the book helped one individual with PC to seek answers, seek God's guidance through prayer, make an intelligent decision, and take the lead in their life, it was well worth the effort on my part.

So, once again I am compelled to thank my lovely wife Sharon for not only suggesting the book but agreeing to read the first pass of the manuscript and suggesting changes. While our children understand how much I appreciated the time they spent at the hospital during my surgery, I want to thank them in print also. Kevin our oldest son and his wife Karen both traveled with us to the hospital and stayed by our sides. Son Kerry lived in a different state but his wife Robyn supported with prayer. Our daughter Kathy who lived in Nebraska called often to check up.

Chuck Watson a good friend and a brother-in-Christ, whom I have never heard complain about any illness, continues to thank me for my suggestions related to his experience with PC and in this he is a true friend. My close friend, whom is always ready to discuss the Word, Larry Turner, at various times he too suggested that I put my articles in book form. In fact he has distributed the articles to friends of his on the other side of the Pond, somewhere in England. Dr. Robert Badalament has to be one of the greatest surgeons I have ever met, and possesses the best of bedside manners.

I must also thank him for his excellent words in the foreword to this book. And I cannot forget another good friend Bill Eddington. Bill is always reliable for recognizing bad grammar.

Another colleague, whom I met while he too was cleaning up his Prostate Cancer act, is Howard Bondy. Howard, a retired English teacher knows how to wield a formidable red marking pen when editing a paper. Howard edited the original articles. Red ink was flowing.

Davisburg
2009

FOREWORD

My brother-in-law, Peter, sent me one of his employees, Jim, for prostate problems. I successfully treated him for prostate cancer, shortly afterwards, Jim returned to work at my brother-in-law's produce market.

When I saw Peter at our next family function, he told me, "You know, Bob, Jim hasn't been the same since he went in to see you."

Remembering how well Jim's treatment had gone, as well as the fact that my brother-in-law is a workaholic, I replied, "Let me guess…these days, Jim's a great employee for eight hours a day, but no longer wants to work twelve hours a day?"

"Exactly," Peter responded.

"You know, Peter," I said, "Getting cancer is a wake-up call. Once you're forced to face your own mortality, your priorities change. Jim no longer cares so much about making as much money as he can. Nowadays, he probably just wants to earn enough cash to pay the bills, and just enjoy the rest of his life."

Prostate cancer changes how you'll live the rest of your life.

As a urologist, I am faced with telling prostate cancer patients the bad news. Typically, I obtain staging studies such as chest x-rays, CT scans and bone scans. Then I sit down with the patient and his family to discuss treatment options.

This is when it gets hard. There are so many treatment options that patients often grow confused and react emotionally rather than rationally.

Often, I tell patients that I'm sometimes faced with two men. Physically, their prostate cancers are identical. Psychologically, their treatment goals are another matter. Some men want surgery. "Cut it out," they'll tell me, and can't wait to schedule radical prostatectomy. Others are frightened by the potential side effects of surgery; these men lean more towards less-invasive procedures such as external beam irradiation, radioactive seed implant, or cryoablation of the prostate.

Different patients have different goals. Some men diagnosed with prostate cancer have been impotent for years. For them, sexual function is a non-issue. Others may have recently remarried to a younger woman, so preservation of sexual function is extremely important.

The night before his surgery, one forty-eight year-old patient told me, "You know, Dr. Badalament, I don't have a college education like you. I own a small store and I have to pick up boxes all day long. If I leak urine every time I pick something up, I won't be able to support my wife and twelve-year-old daughter." Another patient—a lawyer—told me he just couldn't try cases if he had to "face a judge smelling like urine." These patients are very concerned about incontinence.

As a physician, I view myself as the patient's advisor. As in any card game, the patient must play the hand he's dealt. Sometimes, despite the diagnosis of prostate cancer, the prognosis can be another matter entirely. Some patients win "the game," with a measly pair of deuces…others can lose with four aces. As a doctor, I know the odds and want to guide your hand to give you the best possible results.

However, it is impossible for me to accurately assess the patient's quality of life issues…which is to say, how important the patient feels about such matters as avoiding major surgery, preserving urinary control, or sexual function. Many years ago, while serving at Ohio State University, I was doing chart reviews of patients treated by radical prostatectomy.

One patient's chart shocked me. He had a very favorable pathology report and an excellent chance of being cured. Yet he'd fallen so distraught from total urinary incontinence that he'd committed suicide. This taught me the important lesson of how quality-of-life issues need to be factored into treatment decisions.

Recently, one patient told me he wanted to be treated by whatever gave him the best chance of being cured. I asked him to imagine one treatment that was more surgically involved… and had a higher risk of incontinence and impotency as well as surgical risks such as bleeding, strokes, peri-operative heart attacks, or pulmonary embolisms. "Let's assume," I said, "That this treatment option gives you a 70% chance of being cured."

"Now", I continued, "Pretend there is a second option; less invasive, safer, with substantially fewer side effects. This second treatment option has a cure rate of 69%. Which treatment option would you prefer?"

The patient answered, "I'd choose the second treatment option."

"But that isn't what you told me." I reminded him. "You said you wanted the treatment option that offered you the best chance of a cure."

"For just one percent difference, I'd rather take the easier treatment."

I asked the patient if his answer would be the same if the cure rate for the second treatment option was 68%...or 67%, or 66%. "Where would your cut-off be?"

The patient scratched his head, pondering my query. I then answered my own question. "The truth is that the answer will be different for every patient."

Only the patient knows what quality-of-life issues are important for him. Since the survival rates are similar for many of the treatment options, the patient must educate himself to make the best decision for himself. But now the question becomes, where to get the information?

Once you choose your prostate cancer treatment you can't take a mulligan and select another one. If you select radical prostatectomy and find yourself unhappy with it, your prostate can not be put back inside you. Or if your radiation therapy or cryotherapy dissatisfies you, you cannot have your radiation or cryotherapy reversed.

This book, written by my patient Bruce E. Marsee, explores the ways you can help yourself make the "proper" choice. Back in 1998 when he was diagnosed with prostate cancer, Bruce was faced with all the same issues you or one of your loved ones may someday be presented with. To help himself deal with the process, therapeutically, he wrote a series of freelance articles about his experiences with his prostate cancer diagnosis and treatment.

These articles form the basis of this educational and thoughtful discussion of how he "played the hand" fate had dealt him. Use his book as a guide to help you make the best choices for yourself.

Robert A, Badalament, MD
August 23, 2009

TABLE OF CONTENTS

NOT ME

I have always been known to be healthy. God has made sure of that. And too, even as a youth I always held on to the verse of scripture that reads, ***"Honor thy father and thy mother: that thy days may be long upon the land which the Lord thy God giveth thee"*** (Exodus 20:12 KJV).

In fact, prior to 1969, my only disease was the childhood measles and that occurred while growing up in the foothills of southeastern Kentucky. I'm not sure that I went to a doctor. Even back then doctors cost money. Something my family did not have. Come to think of it I don't even remember a doctor's name, during my childhood, to this day. Only the doctor I was named after do I recall, Doctor Bruce Underwood. I was told that Dr. Underwood delivered me on March 8, 1939 at a hospital in Kenvir, Kentucky that was owned and operated by the Black Mountain Coal Company. I do remember eating Jell-O that my Mother prepared for me during the measles illness. It was about the only thing I could eat. And I also recall a large cut in my right foot I received from stepping on a broken Mason Jar. The injury was closed with clamps. I was fooling around in the river, where we kids usually swam, after Mom told me not to go swimming. I went anyway. And I paid dearly for disobeying my Mother. The first step I took was onto that broken glass jar. While trying to run toward my house, as the blood was spurting from the cut, I was screaming God you have got to help me, all the way home. The clamping together of the nasty cut was done by an elderly nurse who worked for the local coal mines. My father paid for her services with a quart of honey, from his beehives.

Then in 1969, at the age of thirty and after a lot of weekend sailing on a local lake, my tonsils became enlarged from being in the water for a lengthy period of time. It was finally suggested by our family doctor that the tonsils be removed. Now in retrospect I think it was a mistake, for a year later the Mumps landed me in the hospital for eight days. I knew God had placed those tonsils in my throat for some reason. I'm now sure the reason was to capture all the bad stuff I was breathing. With the Mumps raging in every part of my body except the pancreas, the Death Angel was knocking at my door. My new doctor informed me later that he thought he was going to lose me. And he had the audacity, at the onset, to tell me I did not need to go to the hospital. He said they probably would not keep me. They would send me back home. Was this doctor ever wrong.

Fortunately I made that call to the hospital and then to the EMS and went anyway. (We had a newborn and for fear of him contracting the Mumps I did not want him around me.) I told the EMS operator just to pick me up, no red lights and no sirens. Since I was unable to walk I was taken by stretcher from my bedroom to the EMS vehicle. After one miserable spinal tap in the hallway of the hospital I spent the first night in the maternity ward. A private room was not available. This was one germ the hospital did not want to spread. I was held in isolation my entire stay. Had I not made that call the grim reaper may have paid me a visit and took me home. One of those visitors, lets say, I did not want to spend time with. Especially with three small children to help rear and be taken care of. I really think they needed a father around the house.

But on the other hand, if God had wanted me I knew he had prepared a better place for me.

Needless to say, I sent the new doctor packing immediately. Since God planned the tonsils to be part of the Lymph Node system, they may have just filtered out the bacteria that caused the Mumps, had they not been removed.

Almost thirty years later at the age of fifty-nine and retired for three years, I was told that I now had Prostate Cancer (PC).

This book will focus on my condition; spiritual, mental, physical, and the prognosis of my PC. We will also touch on the diagnostic procedures, evaluations and treatments as well as the potential side effects, if any, of various medications. Three months later when we were compelled to select either Radiation, Radical Prostatectomy, Cryosurgery or do nothing I will try to explain the rationale behind our decision. Decisions of this nature do not come easy and should be prayed about seeking Gods guidance. Of course it helps when both husband and spouse are on the same team.

We will also review the current body of research that hopefully will assist in the eradication of PC. Support groups, including the Internet will likewise be explored.

There is a world of information and support relative to PC. However, one has to take it upon himself to obtain it. Very few people will offer information freely.

This is one subject that most men do not like to talk about. I don't know why, but that is a fact. I guess it is because most men like to display their macho.

I was one of 244,000 adult males in the United States and one of 8,000 in the state of Michigan that was diagnosed in 1998 with PC, or cancer of the prostate. Surrounding the urethra at the base of the bladder, the prostate is a chestnut shaped organ. Its primary function is to produce seminal liquid, a milky solution that is used as a means of transportation for the sperm. However, I consider myself somewhat lucky because the cancer was detected early. I say "somewhat" for since age forty I had always had an annual PSA exam, so it was not all luck;

I do try to take care of myself.

After all, there is only one me.

And made in the image of God.

Annually more than 27,000 males in the United States are not lucky; they die because the disease was not detected early enough. The irony is that some of these deaths could be prevented if only they would have their PSA tested annually. Actually all could have been prevented had it not been from Adam and Eve back in that garden. And by Noah's time God had to rid the earth of all but seven bodies due to our D&A becoming polluted. Some clinics and hospitals will perform the PSA test for as little as ten dollars. Sometimes the test is perform free of any charges.

PSA or *Prostatic Specific Antigen* is a soluble toxin produced by the prostate organ cells. These toxins are normally carried away by the Lymph Node system and eliminated from the body as waste.

However, an elevation of the PSA in the blood stream indicates that an abnormal cell condition is present. Notice now, *that it indicates an abnormal cell condition is present, not necessarily cancerous.*

I had always understood that the normal range for one's PSA is 0.0 to 4.0, and my PSA had always fallen within the range. However, my PSA in 1995 was 1.5. 1996 it indicated a value of 1.9. In 1997, it was 2.4, and had risen to 3.2 by July 1998.

A closer look at the numbers showed a trend, a trend I became concerned with. Nevertheless, it was within the clinical's published range so I decided to wait and see what my 1999 PSA would indicate.

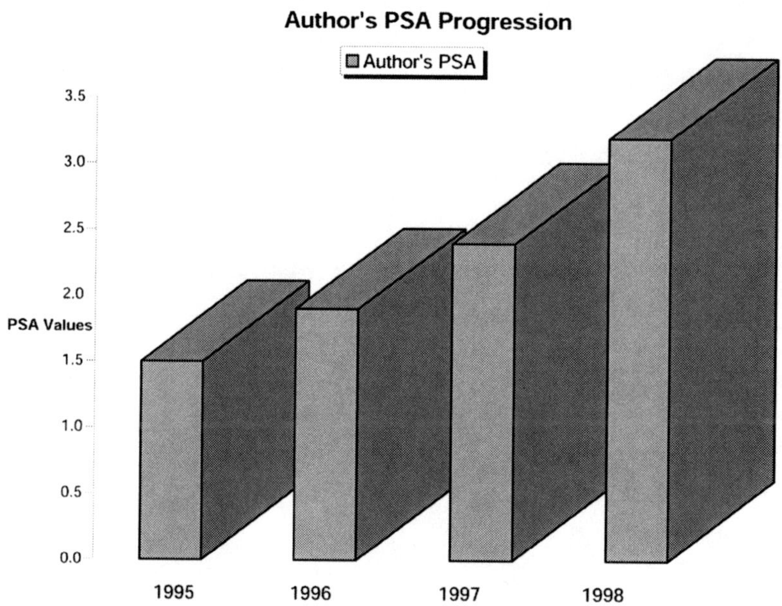

In December of 1998 while scanning a local newspaper I read an article about PC and a new procedure that involved freezing the prostate to a minus 320 degrees. A minus 320 degrees? Now that spiked my interest. The article suggested that a PSA value greater than 3.0 could be a warning sign that cancer might be present. The article went on to say that in addition, one should not rely on PSA alone since 25% of patients with localized prostate cancer have a normal PSA value. With my PSA value at 3.2, I wanted more information and needed to speak with this doctor.

I called for an appointment.

God came through again.

The appointment was scheduled for the next day—December 15, 1998 at Crittenton Hospital in Rochester, Michigan. With the ground white from a recently fallen snow and less than ten days before the holidays, I was to receive a Christmas gift I did not need or want and a "gift" I could not return or exchange.

A CHRISTMAS GIFT

For a reason known only to God, I had read an article about Prostate Cancer (PC) and a new procedure that involved freezing the prostate which at the moment sounded interesting to me. Probably because the doctor featured in the article went on to suggest that a PSA value greater than 3.0 could be a warning sign that cancer might be present. Still, the article continued, one should not rely on PSA alone since 25% of patients with localized prostate cancer have a normal PSA value.

However, an elevation of the PSA in the blood stream indicates that an abnormal cell condition is present. With my PSA value at 3.2, I wanted more information about this procedure and needed to speak with this doctor.

Later I called Crittenton Hospital's Prostate Center in Rochester, Michigan and asked for an appointment with Doctor Fred Lee who was Director of the Prostate Center and had perfected the new Cryosurgery technique. Having been diagnosed with PC some fifteen years earlier, so the article said, Doctor Lee was also a PC survivor. Dr. Lee's technique uses ultrasound, which provides detailed images allowing safe and precise freezing of the prostate to a minus 320 degrees. Now that is mighty cold, cold enough to freeze ones butt off.

My appointment was scheduled for the next day-December 15, 1998.

Since my wife Sharon was still employed, I made the decision to see Doctor Lee alone. I wanted some man-to-man talk. I made my appearance at the hospital early the next morning and was registered rather quickly.

Within a few moments of registration I was escorted to the Prostate Center where I took a seat and waited for my turn with Dr. Lee. I find it to be most interesting what goes on in one's mind as one sits and waits in the hospital waiting room for their turn.

What will the examination include?

Are needles involved?

Will it be painful?

Will my Angel be next to me?

Will I need a second opinion?

I sure hope the insurance covers this sucker.

Gee these nurses are busy. They all seem to be in a rush.

After scanning some of the magazines and speaking with another older gentlemen who is also waiting, it is now my turn.

Dr. Lee's nurse appears from behind a curtain and calls out my name, "Mr. Marsee".

Once in the examining area I recognize Dr. Lee from his picture that was in the paper. Dr. Lee is small in stature and was seated behind a color computer monitor beside the examining table.

After a brief introduction Dr. Lee's nurse holds a small towel in front of me and asks that I lower my slacks and briefs down to my knees and lie on the table.

She continues to hold the towel in front of me while I climb onto the table. Once I am on the soft warm examining table the towel is strategically placed where I have nothing on. In other words, Naked.

I am then instructed to turn onto my left side, bring my knees to my chest in a fetal position, leaving my back to Dr. Lee so that he may do what ever that is he has to do. A second color monitor is located on a table, rather high, and positioned across the room directly in my line of sight. After Dr. Lee inserts the instrument into my body he begins the ultrasound examination. I can see the image of the prostate on the monitor. For several minutes I watch the monitor as Dr. Lee rotates the instrument inside my lower colon and across the prostate.

While I certainly have no medical experience, I do notice something on the monitor that appears different; for some reason it just does not appear to look right. The color is different.

Instinct—maybe?

I say nothing.

The three of us have been doing the usual chitchat that is carried on sometimes during a normal routine exam. Dr. Lee's nurse indicates that she had read an article of mine that appeared in the June, 1998 Issue of Lands' End Catalogue and enjoyed it.

So she said.

Finally, Dr. Lee refers to the monitor I am watching and points out the gray area I was concerned about and says to his nurse that he wants to take a closer look. With this comment, his nurse leaves for a moment and returns with a sterile tray filled with more medical instruments.

There goes that instinct again.

I immediately sense a biopsy is coming.

I am told by Dr. Lee not to move. He informs me that I will feel some pressure and hear a sound similar to a mousetrap, and further assures me there will not be any pain. Sharon keeps reminding me that my pain tolerance is very low, in fact real low. This is one of the senses that God did not bless me with, "A high pain tolerance."

Within a few moments I feel the pressure and hear, "click" and sure enough, something is caught by the mousetrap.

I hear it again.

There it goes again, again and again and again. Finally the last target is seized.

In all, seven biopsies are taken.

I get off the table; sheepishly pull up my briefs and slacks as Dr. Lee's nurse hands me some antibiotics to take for the next three days. She says the antibiotics will prevent any infection that might occur from the biopsies. When the biopsies are taken the needle must break through the colon wall to get at the prostate. Infections can occur.

As I leave the area, I noticed Dr. Lee walking toward the sink with the blood stained needle attached to that intolerable gray molded mousetrap. I think to myself, "I should have stock in that company."

Approximately five o'clock on the 16 of December, 1998 Sharon and I are having a glass of wine while I prepare dinner. (Since retirement I was doing 99% of the cooking-which by the way I enjoyed.)

The phone rings.

Sharon answers and it is Dr. Lee.

She hands the phone to me.

"Mr. Marsee that's cancer", Dr. Lee informs me in a low voice.

Dr. Lee goes on to say the cancer is localized to both nodes of the prostate and should be 100% curable.

With this latest bit of evening news also came some recommendations.

Dr. Lee says his office will schedule a Chest X-ray, a CAT Scan and a Bone Scan to further verify that the cancer has not metastasized. In other words, verify that the cancer is still contained within the Prostate organ and even a single cell has not run amok to infect some other organ. His office will also schedule an appointment with an Urologist for further consultation.

The Urologist will explain various options and start me on a Combination Hormonal Therapy (CHT), the first and mandatory treatment regardless of the initial stage of the disease.

After three or more months of CHT, Sharon and I will select one of the treatments; either a Radical Prostatectomy, Cryosurgery or do nothing…called "Watchful Waiting."

At this point Radiation is out of the question.

It was also suggested that I call PAACT, an organization in Grand Rapids, Michigan that maintains constant research of medical documents and clinical studies on the most advanced methods of detection, diagnostic procedures, evaluation and treatments for PC. PAACT also is committed to furnishing patients, physicians and advocates with the results of these studies.

I hang up the phone, sit down, Sharon and I looked at each other.

I remark, “Now you really know someone who has cancer”.

With Christmas and the celebration of the birth of Christ only nine days away, His was a Christmas present I could not do without and PC was a Christmas present I did not want and one I could never return.

We did a “Toast” to what lies ahead, said our grace and had a great dinner.

CAT SCAN, BONE SCAN AND X-RAYS

December 22, 1998 was a typical winter day in southern Michigan; knee-deep in snow, cold, windy and absolutely miserable. With only three days left before Christmas and the long holidays, the short trip Sharon and I were about to embark upon was not going to be a Christmas shopping trip. Having a PSA of only 3.2 and diagnosed with Prostate Cancer (PC) just seven days' earlier, Dr. Fred Lee's office had scheduled a Bone Scan, CAT Scan and chest X-ray for me.

Dr. Lee was Director of Crittenton's Prostate Center in Rochester, Michigan and has perfected the Cryosurgery technique using color-flow Doppler with ultrasound. The Doppler with ultrasound provides detailed images of the prostate allowing safe and precise freezing of the organ to minus 320 degrees. Thereby, destroying the cancer cells.

A PC option that was only in the experimental stages a few years ago.

Sharon and I arrived at Crittenton Hospital at 7:30 a.m. She had taken the day off from her place of employment to be with me and share the experience. In the thirty-eight years of our marriage we had shared everything and in all probability this was going to be a long day, a day years later we would reminisce about. An event to share with the grandkids, if we ever have any I thought. After all, once we selected the treatment option she too would have to live with the decision.

First on the agenda was a regular chest X-ray. Take everything off above the belt and put on that ugly piece of cloth provided by the hospital.

Then twist your arms out of shape trying to tie the strings of the cloth hanging behind your back. Once that feat is accomplished you sit and wait. Wait while trying to read the outdated and ungodly magazines that are lying about, never knowing what germs the previous readers may have had and left on the dirty pages.

Fortunately, the waiting period was not very long and the X-ray took only a few moments. It was the twisting and holding the breath that was uncomfortable.

Next up was the CAT Scan or a Computerized Axial Tomography also known as CT.

Prior to leaving the house and on the way to the hospital I consumed a “shake” or thirty ounces of liquid dye to make the intestines visible for the CT. It is a white chalky substance one must take prior to having a CAT Scan. CT is a method of combining images from multiple X-rays under the control of a computer to produce cross-sectional or three-dimensional pictures of the internal organs, which then can be used to identify abnormalities.

It is like being able to look inside the body at the internal organs without surgery or an Autopsy. In my case the CT was used to identify any abnormalities and the size of the prostate.

CT is not effective for assessing the stage of PC. The staging is done by a pathologist in a lab using specimens from the biopsy. The CT is significantly more accurate when used for evaluating metastases of the Lymph Nodes or more distant soft tissue sites.

I was instructed by the technician to lie (fully clothed) on the flat table of the CT apparatus with my right arm extended above my head. An IV was inserted into my right arm to allow a dye solution to enter my body. As it began to flow into the vein I started to feel very warm inside. The sensation was taking place while the table slowly moved me through the inside of the CT scanner, much like going through the middle of a "doughnut". When a small overhead light came on, I was to hold my breath until it disappeared. Fortunately the light was on for only a few seconds.

Pain, claustrophobia—none what-so-ever.

Once off the CT table I was told to proceed to the Nuclear Medicine room for the final test. Within the Nuclear Medicine room is where the Bone Scan takes place. The Bone Scan is a technique much more sensitive than conventional X-rays. This scan uses a radioactive isotope to identify abnormal or cancerous growths within or attached (attached here is the key word) to the bone. In the case of PC, a bone scan is used to identify bony metastases which are definitive for cancer that has escaped from the prostate and appear as "hot spots" on the film.

However, the absence of' hot spots do not prove the absence of tiny metastases. While hot spots frequently occur along the spine, ribs and skull the spine is the most common site outside the prostate for prostate cancer growth.

Prior to having a bone scan, the radioactive isotope is injected into the bloodstream.

The small vile containing the isotope is kept in a secured, insulated metal box and opened only when the technician is ready to give the injection. Once injected the patient has a three-hour wait period before undergoing the bone scan. The waiting period allows the isotope to circulate throughout the body and be absorbed by the bones.

It was around noon that my injection was given so Sharon and I left the hospital planning to have lunch and take in some shopping. After doing lunch and walking for exercise, I purchased a few bottles of wine. I like to cook with wine and have a glass or two while I am preparing a meal. After all, containing antioxidants a couple of glasses of red wine a day is good for the body, so they say. In fact I think it is interested what the Prophet Isaiah had to say in Isaiah chapter 25 verse 6. ***"And in this mountain shall the Lord of hosts make unto all people a feast of fat things, a feast of wines on the lees, of fat things full of marrow, of wines on the lees well refined."*** (KJV) When we do research on the word "Lees" it means well bodied and aged wine. A beverage that would not be found in your local wine shop.

Once back at the hospital it was time to lie on the Bone Scan table and go through another doughnut, but the middle of this doughnut was longer and took considerable more time. In fact, movement of the body while being scanned is a no-no and the doughnut moves very slowly. While scanning the pelvic area, the equipment is quite close to the body.

As with the CT procedure I experienced no pain nor was I claustrophobic.

Later in the afternoon, it was finally time to return home and wait for someone to call with the results. December 23, Dr. Lee called and informed us that the results was negative, however there was a spot on my right lung and he suggested another X-ray for comparison.

I had previously had a portable chest X-ray taken in 1996 and Dr. Lee mentioned the spot was probably just a fluke. Fortunately after the follow-up X-ray and a comparison, that is exactly what it turned out to be; a fluke and nothing to worry about.

With all the testing concluded, an appointment with the Urologist was scheduled to place everything in proper perspective with help of the Partin tables. The PSA numbers, results of the DRE, Biopsy, Gleason score, X-rays, CAT Scan and Bone Scan would all be compiled to help assist in the best treatment as well as suggest some options. These options Sharon and I would have to consider and pray about in the next few months.

Whatever option we choose, and no matter what happen, Sharon will have to watch it from the sidelines. For the cancer is in me, not her. But after the Urologist visit we will need a break—some vacation time in one of our favorite locations—CANCUN Mexico. With a bag full of material on PC we did a lot of reading and studying, including digesting the magazine PAACT that Dr. Lee suggested we subscribe to. A week later we arrived back home from CANCUN rested and ready, with God's help, to tackle the cancer that had invaded my body.

THE UROLOGIST

The January snow continued to fall as I maneuvered the car into the Medical Building parking lot behind Crittenton Hospital in Rochester, Michigan.

My appointment was originally scheduled for the previous day but with the snowstorm and whiteouts it had to be rescheduled for 3 p.m., January 14, 1999. Instructions were for me to take the elevator to the fourth floor of the Medical Building and continue down the long corridor to suite 420. Having been recently diagnosed with Prostate Cancer (PC), today I was to speak with one of the surgeons who would help guide me through the next few months of uncertainly. A mountain I had never climbed or a stream I had never traversed. It is during periods of time like this that Psalm 23:4 comes to mind. ***"Yea, though I walk through the valley of the shadow of death, I will fear no evil: for thou art with me; thy rod and thy staff they comfort me"***. After glancing at all the nameplates and room numbers I spot one that reads, "420—Dr. Robert Badalament—Urologist".

Since this was my first visit with Dr. Badalament I sign in, present my identification, insurance cards, find a seat in the waiting room and fill out the medical history and insurance forms.

The light colored walls are decorated with paintings by the artist Thomas Kincad. While Kincad has a unique way of painting outdoor scenes and cottages, I find them a little too brilliant for my taste. They almost appear to be massed produced.

I prefer the more subtle scenes painted by Paul Sawyier.

Mr. Sawyier was from Kentucky. My native land.

While glancing through a series of magazines a side door to the waiting room opens, catches my attention, and a young lady attired in a nurses uniform motions for me to come with her.

Tracy, Dr. Badalament's nurse introduces herself and directs me to one of the nearby examination rooms. Wouldn't you know it; Kincade's pictures are all over the walls. However, the top of the cabinet work area has items more interesting; molded models of the male prostate and other internal organs. I am fascinated by these models. Is that really what I look like inside? I pick up a model of the prostate organ and rub my finger over the plastic. You can feel the lump, as would the doctor during a Digital Rectal Exam, or DRE. And God made man in His image! One thing I am sure of, God does not need all of these organs, maybe when He was on earth.

After taking my blood pressure and pulse, Tracy informs me that the pressure is 140 over 80, a little higher than usual and the pulse; 84. The white coat syndrome I say to myself quietly. She then proceeds to ask family history questions. Then personal questions and if that is not enough; intimate questions.

Some very intimate.

When I respond to one question, “Paula Jones could answer a question like that”, a laughing Tracy reply, “everyone says that”.

Tracy completes her part of the examination and leaves the room as a pleasant, smiling Dr. Robert Badalament enters, still in surgical blues. A quick greeting is exchanged and we get down to business, after all; I am not a passive patient and I have a list of questions that I printed prior to leaving home. I want answers. Real honest to goodness, man to man answers. This is my life not Dr. Badalaments. My well earned dollars as well as the insurance companies are paying good money for this treatment and advice.

For the next hour Dr. Badalament and I discuss the PC growing inside my body and my prognoses.

According to Dr. Badalament and the lab reports my cancer is diploid; having one complete set of normally paired chromosomes, i.e., a normal amount of DNA. The cancer is a six on the Gleason score, which indicates its growth, is moderate and will double in size approximately every four years. Using the Partin Tables which predicts the pathological stage of localized Prostate Cancer, Dr. Badalament concludes that the combination of my PSA (3.2), Clinical Stage (T1C, by Ultrasound) and Gleason Score (6) predicts the following; it is confined to the prostate with a seventy-eight percent chance it will stay confined. In other words, there is a little better than twenty-percent chance the cancer will penetrate the prostate wall and enter the blood system.

Reviewing the Partin tables further with Dr. Badalament showed there is only a one-percent chance the cancer will involve the Seminal Vesicle. These glands, located at the base of the bladder, are connected to the prostate and provide nutrients for the semen—the fluid emitted at ejaculation containing both the semen and the sperm. While it is often referred to as semen the proper wording would be ejaculate. Ninety-nine percent of the ejaculate is Seminal Vesicle fluid, which is rich in fructose, and prostate fluid. The fructose provides a high-energy source required by the sperm while swimming a marathon race and entering a hostile environment.

There is zero to one percent chance that the cancer will also involve the Lymph Nodes. Currently I would say pretty good odds; the type you bet on.

Even though the cancer is very small at this stage and cannot be felt via a DRE (Digital Rectal Exam); it can still be very deadly if left unchecked. For completely eliminating this nuisance, and it is only a nuisance, Sharon and I have completely turned the situation over to God. Dr. Badalament and I agree on two options. (Sharon and I have ruled out Radiation with the prognosis, my age and health. Plus, my trust in Radiation is zero.)

The first option was a Radical Prostatectomy, an operation to remove the entire prostate organ and Seminal Vesicles. (Dr. Badalament had just completed two radicals—the reason for surgical blues.)

Cost was approximately $25,000.

The hospital stay can be anywhere from two to five days with a catheter inserted for the next three weeks. Follow up can last for the next few years.

Possible side effects are; risk of impotence, incontinence and complications after surgery.

The downside of a radical; should the surgeon cut through or disturb the cancer while removing the prostate from the base of the bladder, the cancer can spread. Once the cancer is removed, there are no other options, with the exception of Radiation or Chemotherapy.

My other option was Cryosurgery; the use of liquid nitrogen probes to freeze the prostate to a minus 320 degrees to kill the cancerous cells, including any cancerous tissue. Cost was approximately $13,000 with an overnight hospital stay and an inserted catheter for the next three weeks. Follow up for the next five years includes intervals of biopsies.

Possible side effects are; the cancer may not be destroyed, risk of impotence and disturbance of the urinary function. On the positive side, Cryosurgery can be repeated and a patient would continue to have other options.

For the next few months, Dr. Badalament places me on a Combination Hormonal Therapy (CHT), the first and mandatory treatment regardless of the initial stage of the disease.

CHT includes Casodex—a small white tablet that block the conversion of testosterone produced by the testicles and adrenal glands (adrenal glands too produce a small amount of testosterone), into Dihydrotestosterone (DHT). In prostate cancer, DHT stimulates the cancer cells' uncontrolled growth.

CHT also includes Proscar—a small blue tablet that blocks the formation of DHT in the prostate. When DHT is removed, the prostate shrinks in size.

Both medications are to be taken daily.

I was to return five days later January 19, 1999 for a Zoladex implant which was also part of the CHT regiment. This small capsular implanted in the abdomen will cause the brain to send a signal to the Testicles for the next three months, instructing them to stop producing testosterone. In other words, I would have to learn to live with chemically induced celibacy.

The five-day interval between the visit January 14, and January 19, was to provide the medication Casodex the ability to shut down the conversion of testosterone by the adrenal glands. Were testosterone to be shut down by the testicles first, the adrenal glands would only step up the production of testosterone. Something I did not need at this stage of the game.

I walk out of the office with a handful of sample drugs, two prescriptions, and Dr. Badalament's business card with an appointment scheduled for March 29, 1999 and written answers to my questions.

As I walk out of the building and toward the parking lot to my car, I knew God was walking with me. Nevertheless; I shake my head and think, "what a way to start 1999".

THE RADIOLOGIST

Sharon and I were waiting outside Dr. Lee's office when he arrived at 7:45 a.m.

We had braved the cold and windy Michigan morning to speak with Dr. Fred Lee, a radiologist and Director of Crittenton Hospital's Prostate Center. My appointment had been scheduled for January 19, in regard to the Prostate Cancer (PC) I had been diagnosed with the previous month. The consultation was to be followed-up in the afternoon with another chest X-ray and an abdomen implant of Zoladex, which had been prescribed by Dr. Badalament, my Urologist, earlier in the month.

Approximately fifteen years ago Dr. Lee, too, had been diagnosed with PC, however, his PC had found its way into the lymph nodes.

He was given five years to live.

That was in 1984.

After a two-year sabbatical and devoting his time to researching early diagnosis of PC, Dr. Lee is now a pioneer in the field of early detection of PC using transrectral ultrasonography (TRUS) with color flow Doppler (CFD). (Even as I update the articles for this book in 2009, Dr. Lee is still practicing as a Radiologist. He has since left Crittenton and joined the practice of Dr. Badalament.)

Dr. Lee defined what PC looked like in transrectal ultrasound and his work has lead to its widespread acceptance as the preferred method of diagnosing PC. In 1999, the International College of Surgeons awarded Dr. Lee with an "Honorary Fellowship." He is the first radiologist in history to receive this distinction. Dr. Lee is also one of the team members that helped guide me through a valley of uncertainty. And it was also Dr. Lee who with his early diagnosis found the cancers that had invaded the privacy of my body.

Dr. Lee is a very soft-spoken person and is intensely precise in his explanations. As Sharon and I listened, he illustrated to us on paper the stages of prostate cancer. He wanted to make sure that we both understood what was taking place inside my body, especially inside the prostate, and what my treatment options were. He also tells of a close friend and surgeon that he lost to PC.

He wanted to know if we had any questions.

I had a myriad of questions and I have always encouraged Sharon to ask questions. After all, we are partners in love and life. Additionally, she may have to function as my 24-hour nurse should problems develop after the treatment.

According to Dr. Lee, the results of his TRUS with CFD and biopsy, the lab reports, my PSA and other data indicated that the location of my cancer is in the right and left base of the prostate.

In other words, I have two cancers.

Their sizes are 1.5mm and 6mm respectively.

Small, but potentially deadly.

Rather than aggressive they are moderate in their growth. The probability of their penetrating the prostate wall and entering the lymph nodes are very slim, in fact only two percent.

While Dr. Lee's specialty is Cryosurgery (freezing the prostate to a minus three hundred and twenty degrees) he explained and detailed other treatment options.

The first option was a Radical Prostatectomy—an operation to remove the entire prostate organ and seminal vesicles.

Option two was Radiation Therapy—the use of X-rays and other forms of Radiation to destroy malignant cells and tissue.

And number three was Cryosurgery.

The second option we immediately ruled out because of my age, excellent health and potential damage to other internal organs that can result from Radiation. At this stage of the game, I did not want my body to receive massive doses of Radiation. If I am already sick with cancer why would I want to be burned? After all, many doctors believe that Radiation only "stuns" the bad cells, and there are cells that could escape, especially if the doses and the focusing of the Radiation are not absolutely accurate.

Even though nothing is guaranteed, Dr. Lee said my cure rate is close to 100%. This is because my PC was detected at an early stage with my PSA at 3.2.

As Dr. Lee explained, often times when the PSA reaches 4.0 the cancer has penetrated the prostate capsule and spread into the lymph nodes. This is a further incentive for men to have a TRUS with CFD anytime their PSA level proceeds to trend upward.

He went on to illustrate why it is so important for women to have mammograms. Once a lump is felt, often times it is too late.

The cancer has spread.

Only the TRUS and CFD for the prostate and Mammogram for the breast can detect the early stages of cancer. However, this too depends on how accurately the test is read.

Before Sharon and I left Dr. Lee's office, he handed Sharon the paper he had been writing on. (See appendix.) He then instructed his secretary to make a copy of all records and lab reports pertaining to my PC and give them to us. He also made sure I had a copy of the latest study he had participated in and had presented in, "Seminars in Urologic Oncology, August 1998". After spending some time in conversation with Dr. Lee, one soon comes to the realization that here is a man truly dedicated to his work, and to the well being of his fellow man.

I drove Sharon to her office, then returned to the hospital where another chest X-ray was taken, (which turned out to be negative,) and went to have the Zoladex Implant.

After an injection of Lidocaine, a numbing agent, the small capsule was implanted into my abdomen, leaving a nasty bruise the size of a half-dollar.

For the next three months as the little capsule dissolves, it will send a signal to the brain instructing the testicles to stop producing testosterone.

Finally—just finally—I was done with insurance forms, examinations, needles, X-rays, consultations, charts, driving, sitting and waiting while scanning those awful magazines.

Now while on Combination Hormonal Therapy (CHT), the first and mandatory treatment regardless of the initial stage of the disease, Sharon and I could read, research and speak with others who had encountered PC and chart my progress. Moreover, we would do some of this while Sharon and I cruise the Grecian Isles.

In the weeks that followed, after praying for some direction from God, weighing the risks and the long term benefits, Sharon and I would select one of the treatment options that we both felt would be most appropriate for my condition. One we both would be comfortable with. But now lets just enjoy life and each other while we visit Athens, Rhodes, Ephesus and other sites where the Apostle Paul journeyed and spread the Gospel of our Lord and Savior Jesus the Christ.

MEDICATION & SIDE EFFECTS

I have never been one who feels they must belong to an organization, or any group for that matter, just to fill my days and evenings with something to do, or someplace to go. I have plenty to do even if it is just reading, writing or singing Southern Gospel in Church. However, since being diagnosed with Prostate Cancer (PC) in December 1998 I definitely now belong to a group. A very, very large group

I was one of the 8,000 male victims in the state of Michigan who was diagnosed with PC in 1998. As the hours turned into days, days into weeks and the weeks into months, I accepted the fact that I was a cancer victim. At no time did I ever say or even think, "Oh woe is me, I have Cancer". On the other hand I prefer to think of PC as more of a nuisance. I will get over this; it is just a matter of time. On the other hand—if God wants to take me home, I'm ready. Remember, ***"After all death is only a comma, not a period".***

Once the ordeal was over, I advanced to an opposing group called, "Cancer Survivors."

January 19, 1999, Dr. Badalament started me on a daily Combination Hormonal Therapy (CHT). CHT includes Casodex—a small white tablet that blocks the conversion of testosterone produced by the adrenal glands (adrenal glands also produce a small amount of testosterone) into

Dihydrotestosterone (DHT) and Proscar—a small blue tablet that blocks the formation of DHT in the prostate.

In PC, DHT stimulates the cancer cells' uncontrolled growth. Removing DHT or the stimulation shrinks the prostate and starves the cancer cells.

There was also a small Zoladex capsule, implanted in my abdomen, which instructed the brain to send a signal to the testicles instructing them to stop producing testosterone for the next three months. It takes the entire three months for this small capsule to completely dissolve into the blood stream.

On Saturday January 23, five days after the Zoladex tablet implant, I began to have flu like symptoms with aches and pains. (Possible side effects according to the printed documentation.) Accompanying this was nasal congestion, sinus pressure, back pain but no fever. Around midnight I finally had a sweat-out and felt somewhat better the next day.

The following Monday I continued to feel bad enough to place a call to my urologist Dr. Robert Badalament, to verify if this was a CHT side effect. I was feeling so miserable that my son and his wife, feeling sorry for me, cleared the snow from our long driveway. Something I normally enjoy doing myself. After all this is about all the exercise I get in the winter.

With only four days until we were supposed to leave for Cancun, I had started on my second box of tissue. Finally, I took an Alka-Seltzer and slept the afternoon away.

Later Monday evening Dr. Badalament returned my call.

For the next hour we discussed Prostate Cancer, the articles I was writing, family, and colleges (Ohio State his alma mater). Dr. Badalament also informed me that he was offered a position with Memoral Sloan-Kettering in New York following his fellowship in 1987. In 1995 he came to Crittenton Hospital in Rochester, Michigan.

Although I felt miserable I also felt I was in good hands as he called in a prescription of Zithromax, a powerful antibiotic, to our local Pharmacist.

By the time Sharon and I arrived at the airport in Cancun I was so tired that standing in line for an extended period of time holding our passports did not make me impatient. I was just another robot. By dinnertime, totally exhausted and with a flushed face, I was not interested in the appealing dinner set before me.

Forget about the waves crashing against the beach of white soft sand.

I went to bed.

After finishing the last three capsules of Zithromax in Cancun, my old self begin to come around. Whether this setback was a side effect of Zoladex, CHT in general, or the common flu, we will never know. Nevertheless, it was good to get it over with.

However, periodically and almost instantly, I would be completely wiped-out. The resulting reaction to all the medication I would contend with for a while longer.

One definite side effect I found with Zoladex was an increase in my appetite. In fact, I weigh a little more than I did prior to the implant, and it was not the result of staying indoors which was caused by all the snow fall we had the winter of 1998.

Hot flashes—I had my share of them, too, and believe me; they are not so bad during the cold winter nights.

Crying for no apparent reason was something else.

Growing up in the foothills of Southeastern Kentucky I have never considered myself to be a very emotional person. It takes a lot to upset me enough to produce tears. However, that little Zoladex capsule can cause tears to flow, but at least you know why they are flowing.

With Proscar, a finasteride, it attacks the potency. Forget about one's libido—it is nonexistent. All the beautiful models in the world could strip down bare butt, but while taking this very small tablet you would quietly request they put their clothes back on. There is absolutely no sex appeal by the other gender.

During the entire period of writing the articles, I encountered no side effects that I could attribute to Casodex, a bicalutamide. While it is said to cause high blood pressure, itching of skin (maybe a little of this) mental depression, anemia, short-term memory loss (I have always had this) and other side effects, I felt none of them.

Still with the significant fall in serum testosterone these symptoms never showed up even after six months on CHT. I say six months because I chose to stay on CHT for a six-month period, meaning I got another injection at the three months interval.

I did not intend to exceed the six months on this medication. Plus, I wanted to make sure both cancers had shrunk in size.

On the positive side, most of the side effects can be treated with a proper diet, vitamins, exercise, and prescribed drugs to help maintain one's overall health.

I found that I could control the hot flashes with soy products. The milk is very tasty, especially on cereal. I no longer purchase the soy chocolate milk because one drink and it is all gone. It is just that good.

Tofu takes on the flavor of whatever it is prepared with. It is excellent when prepared with a vegetable stir-fry. And I found Soy Hot Dogs and Soy Cheese not to be that bad.

Annually since 1984, I have paid a visit to Dr. Ned Winkelman, a plastic surgeon, who removes small skin tabs from my neck area. All of these tabs have been benign until 1999. I neglected to have one removed in 1998. While this particular skin tab grew during 1998 and 1999, while in Cancun I noticed that it began to shrink as I continued with CHT.

Upon returning home and being concerned I immediately scheduled an appointment with Dr. Winkelman for a biopsy. Two days after my visit with Dr. Winkelman his secretary called and informed me the biopsy was Squamous Cell Carcinoma, not melanoma and not likely to spread but it should be taken off.

On Thursday, February 18, and 18 stitches later it was off.
Once again a fine job by Dr. Winkelman.
No scaring and the injection are like little needle pricks.

I often told Dr. Winkelman that it was almost a pleasure getting an injection from him.

With PC inside me and Squamous Cell Carcinoma on my neck, I questioned Dr. Winkelman as to a correlation. Dr. Winkelman's explanation: Squamous Cell Carcinoma is seen primarily in older patients (I'm was sixty at the time.), mostly men. Like Basal Cell Carcinoma, its prime cause factor is solar Radiation.

Hereditary factors are important also.

While there is not a known direct correlation between the shrinking of the Squamous Cell Carcinoma and CHT, my urologist stated, "You may be on to something," when I informed him.

On the flip side of the coin, statistics have shown that if a diagonal line was drawn from California on the West Coast to the Carolinas on the East Coast, those males residing north of the line are more subjected to PC then those males living south of the line. It is said that the body requires at least fifteen minutes of sunlight daily without sunscreen. Sunlight helps to manufacture Vitamin D required by this wonderful body of ours. And most males do not get enough sunlight.

As is readily apparent I am not a passive patient. I believe in taking my health care into my own hands. If ever there was a reason to become an educated consumer, PC is one.

After all, I am the one who has to live the life, not the radiologist, the urologist, the physician or the surgeon.

I am also the one who is left to pay what the insurance company does not cover; therefore, I will also call the shots.

DECISION TIME

One would think when a cancer victim spends six months becoming an educated patient on Prostate Cancer (PC) by reading, researching, speaking with other PC victims and survivors, making a decision for treatment would be rather easy. Especially with the support of their spouse.

Believe me it is not.

Because the long-range side effects are very similar between Cryosurgery and Radical prostatectomy, making the decision between the two did not come easy. Vacillating between the Radical Prostatectomy (complete removal of the prostate) and Cryosurgery (turning the prostate into an ice ball at minus 320 degrees) it was time to resolve the uncertainty and make a decision, a decision that could not be postponed any longer.

It is at moments like this that ignorance could be bliss.

Having been diagnosed with PC in December, 1998, and spending six months on Combination Hormonal Therapy (CHT), the first and mandatory treatment regardless of the initial stage of the disease, it was time to rid myself of the medication and the cancer and get on with my life. Supposedly after six months of CHT the cancer cells have shrunk by fifty percent. At least that is what they told me.

After surgery we were to find out.

During my own clinical adventures, I accompanied my young son and his wife to the Mayo Clinic. Spending twelve days in Rochester, Minnesota provided me with the opportunity to visit Mayo Clinic's cancer information area and further increase my knowledge of PC. The Mayo Clinic treats over one and one-half million patients a year, a good many of those with PC.

The time spent with my son also provided me the opportunity to discuss PC with him and his wife. Now that I am a cancer victim, one of our son's has a one hundred-percent chance that one-day they too will become victims. Research has shown that fathers who have sons and who are diagnosed with PC will pass the PC gene down to one of his male offspring. Which in my case means that each of my two sons now have a fifty-percent chance of being diagnosed, sometime during their life span, with PC. A sobering thought for parents.

While there are certainly very good clinics and hospitals in most major metropolitan areas, we found that Mayo Clinic was the place to go for a prompt diagnosis. Especially when it involves the gallbladder, as it turned out to be my son's medical problem. He had spent many a painful hour in many a hospital throughout the United States without receiving the correct diagnosis. The excellent staff at Mayo Clinic solved it after only a few visits and tests.

Later while vacationing in Greece and Turkey, Sharon and I met and spoke with an urologist from Kentucky. During one of our many conversations, and after learning of my PC, he asked my age.

When I told him sixty, he responded that if I were seventy he would suggest that I do nothing. That is called watchful—

waiting. However, since I was only sixty and in excellent health, his suggestion was that I have the prostate surgically removed. Coming from an urologist, who has been practicing for over thirty years, it sounded like good advice—but advice I was not ready for.

While undergoing a routine colonoscopy I was also surprised to hear the same advice coming from my proctologist Dr. Farouk Tootla during our discussion on Radical Prostatectomy versus Cryosurgery. He had undergone a Radical in 1998. Although he experienced a collapsed lung during surgery, caused by improper administering of the anesthesia, he said, Dr. Tootla continues to believe that the radical is the "Gold Standard" and is the only way to go. He too is quite young, in good health, has a positive outlook, and a very successful medical practice.

Eventually one aspect of Cryosurgery did help me in arriving at a decision. Currently Cryosurgery requires five years of biopsies as a follow-up. Nine biopsy's over five years (more than fifty-four single needle punctures in what would be left of my prostate) would be required after Cryosurgery. One needle puncture certainly does not appeal to me, let alone over fifty-four. And since the tissue around the urethra and other areas of the prostate are not frozen, (only where the cancer resides) the potential exists for the return of the cancer in the remaining tissue.

Of course follow-up Cryosurgery can be performed if needed. In any event, one lives with the certainty of biopsies and the possibility of the return of PC.

The final incentive for the decision came as I was leaving the home of a friend. He was in his eighties, a gifted musician and artist, and had recently suffered a small stroke. As we talked, he informed me that he was having some lower back pain and problems urinating, which I understand to be a probable sign of prostate trouble.

Saying good by and walking to my car, I kept thinking to myself that if I do not get that little sucker (prostate) removed I could one day be experiencing the same symptoms. By the time I reached my car the decision, on my part, had been made. Once in my car I immediately call Dr. Badalament and told him "Bob, that sucker has to come out. All the way. Leave nothing behind." Driving home I kept telling myself that the prostate had to come out—not frozen, not radiated, but completely removed. And this was one decision I knew Sharon would agree with.

As Sharon and I viewed many educational videos produced and distributed by large pharmaceutical firms, it became more obvious to us that PC is a "we" disease: While the tumor obviously is not shared, everything that accompanies PC is: the doctor visits, the support group meetings, the uncertainty of what lies ahead, trying to understand the cause and effect on relationships, and making the treatment option decision.

June 18, 1999 I met with my urologist, Dr. Robert Badalament and once again informed him of our decision. We discussed the surgery and post surgery; wearing of a Foley catheter for three weeks, no driving for six weeks, and also the potential side effects: impotence, incontinence and blood clotting.

Since the decision had now been made for a Radical Prostatectomy I asked Dr. Badalament what his success rate was and had he lost any patients. He informed me that, "yes" he had lost one patient. It seems after returning home from surgery and a short hospital stay the patient did not do the walking as he was instructed. Consequently, a blood clot was formed leading to the patient's death. Sharon took the information to heart. And walk. Did I ever walk.

On June 24, I went through pre-admission at Crittenton Hospital with blood taken, chest X-ray and electrocardiogram. I spoke with the anesthesiologist and discussed the anesthesia and the placement of the epidural (I also suggested that he keep me under until August. I have always commented that I could go to sleep just before Thanksgiving and sleep until the day after New Years.) Prior to my leaving the hospital, a nurse gave me a plastic jug full of powder that I was to mix with water the day prior to surgery. Once cooled, the gallon of cherry flavored liquid was to be consumed within four hours. I was to be one clean individual when I checked in for surgery the following day, July 6, 1999.

Now that was a challenge!

To be placed with my medical files in the hospital I left a copy of my Living Will, giving Sharon the right to tell the doctor not to prolong my life under certain conditions. While Sharon does not like for me to talk about death it does happen during surgery, sometimes. Since a Radical Prostatectomy is no minor surgery, I like to prepare for the worst-case scenario. I wanted to make it clear that I did not want to be kept alive by extraordinary or artificial means.

In addition, I did not want to be revived if it was certain that I was dying. In jest I told Sharon that if they did try to revive me and I lived I would have an attorney sue the Doctor, Hospital and the staff.

Additionally this is not something that can be left for the last moment, unless you know the final outcome.

Once the decision had been made to have the radical, I immediately begin to prepare myself both physically and psychologically for the surgery. A regiment of exercise to build up my muscle mass included arm and leg curls. Since a patient can lose up to five units of blood during a Radical Prostatectomy, a daily intake of 320 mg of slow releasing iron tablets was included in my daily diet. I was not interested in a blood transfusion at any stage of the game.

I also continued taking vitamins E, C and Flax Seed.

To improve my chances of remaining continent, I began the Kegels, or exercising the urethral sphincter muscle at the base of the prostate. This is the muscle that keeps the urine inside the bladder. It can be exercised by stopping the urine in mid stream or by flexing the muscle while sitting or walking. It can even be exercised while driving a car. (After surgery it would be located at the base of the bladder.)

All of this preparation was to pay big dividends post surgery. (One would be surprised at the PC victims who neglected this simple exercise and who later complained after surgery of being incontinent.)

SURGERY & RECOVERY

July 6, 1999, Sharon and I were up early. Real early.

Sleeping is difficult when you know you are facing major surgery the next day.

At the home of our son and his wife, five houses from our home, they were in the process of making coffee, strong coffee. Of course that is the only way Kevin will drink it—Strong. This was a day the four of us would not soon forget. Having been diagnosed with Prostate Cancer in December 1998, today the bad body parts would be removed. Destroyed. My surgery was scheduled for 10:45am with urologist and surgeon Dr. Robert Badalament. Badalament is noted for his research on cancer and has authored over one hundred medical articles. I felt God would be guiding the hands of Dr. Badalament as our caravan of two cars headed for Crittenton Hospital in Rochester, Michigan. Approximately a thirty to forty minute drive from our homes.

After going through the process of being admitted, I was directed to a prep area where I disrobed and once again put on that ugly thing of a gown. (I had already provided the hospital with my Living Will, giving Sharon the right to tell the doctor not to prolong my life under certain circumstances. I wanted to make it clear that I did not want to be kept alive by extraordinary or artificial means. And I did not want to be revived if it was certain that I was dying.) Since a Radical

Prostatectomy is no minor surgery I wanted to prepare for the worst-case scenario.

A few moments after the gown was finally secured a nurses-aide entered my private curtain area and begin to shave the part of the abdomen where the Radical Prostatectomy was to be performed. A place where only one's spouse views. I was then given a mild sedative. The anesthesiologist who would place the epidural in my back and along the spine arrived soon thereafter. After almost passing out during the insertion process, with my head resting on Sharon's shoulder, the epidural was finally inserted. However, our son Kevin did have to leave the area. With all the surgeries he has endured Kevin continues to dislike hospitals. The epidural is intended to control the pain during and after surgery, and it would be left in place for approximately three days. I was also informed by the anesthesiologist that there was a fifty-percent chance that the epidural might not work. (Only later did I realize the significance of this statement.)

At the appointed time, after saying my good-byes to the family and giving Sharon a kiss a nurse rolled the gurney I was very comfortable on into surgery room number one. It was action time. The bright lights were glaring and the stage was set. The last thing I recall, as the curtain came down over my face, was Dr. Badalament standing stage left, rolling up and taping a long object. (Later I learned the object was placed under my spine to arch my body upward.) Once in never-never land a Foley catheter was inserted into the penis and up through the urethra and positioned in the bladder. This would aid in the removal of the prostate.

Dr. Badalament then proceeded to make an eight-inch incision below my navel, all the way to the pubis. Before the prostate organ was reached, the left and right lymph nodes were removed and immediately sent to the pathologist. If they are free of cancer cells, the surgeon continues the surgery. Should the report come back positive, the surgery will be stopped and the incision closed.

The lymph nodes are a "free system" and appears almost like a large mesh screen covering the entire body; consequently, cancer cells can be carried and circulated throughout the body if the nodes have been invaded.

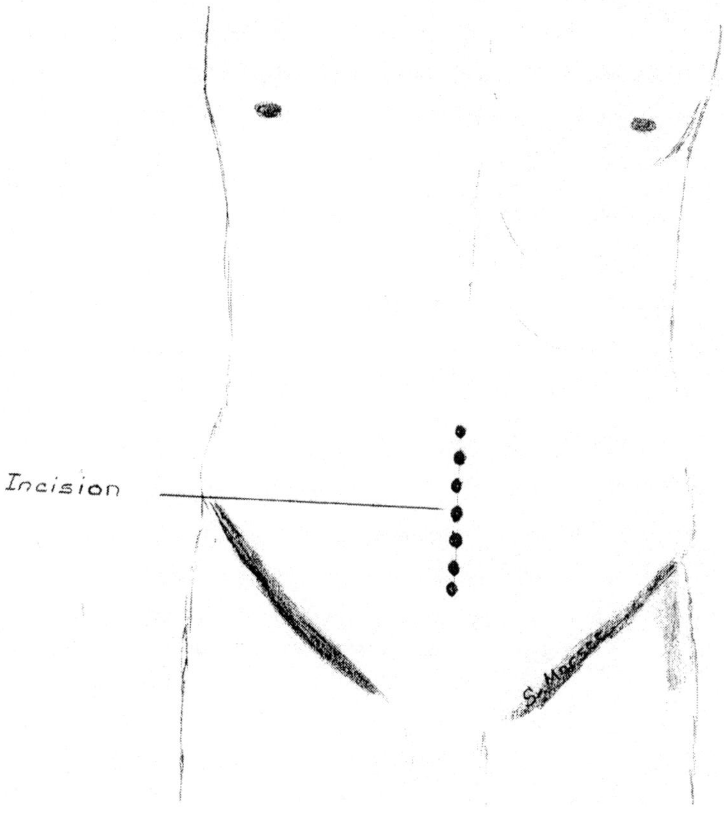

Having been informed by the pathologist that the lymph nodes showed no signs of cancer, Dr. Badalament, with his hands now inside my abdomen, continues with the surgery.

In order to maintain a bloodless field to operate in, the Dorsal Venus Complex, a large group of veins located over the top of the prostate and extending down the sides must be separated and tied to obtain full exposure of the organ. (While viewing an X-ray eight years later the titanium staples were still visible where Dr. Badalament had stapled off the veins. See Appendices.) Should these veins be accidentally severed, Dr. Badalament would have to perform the surgery in a pool of blood and race against the clock. And the clock does not slow, even for major surgery.

Next the tendon that attaches the urethra to the pubic bone area is cut, freeing the urethra.

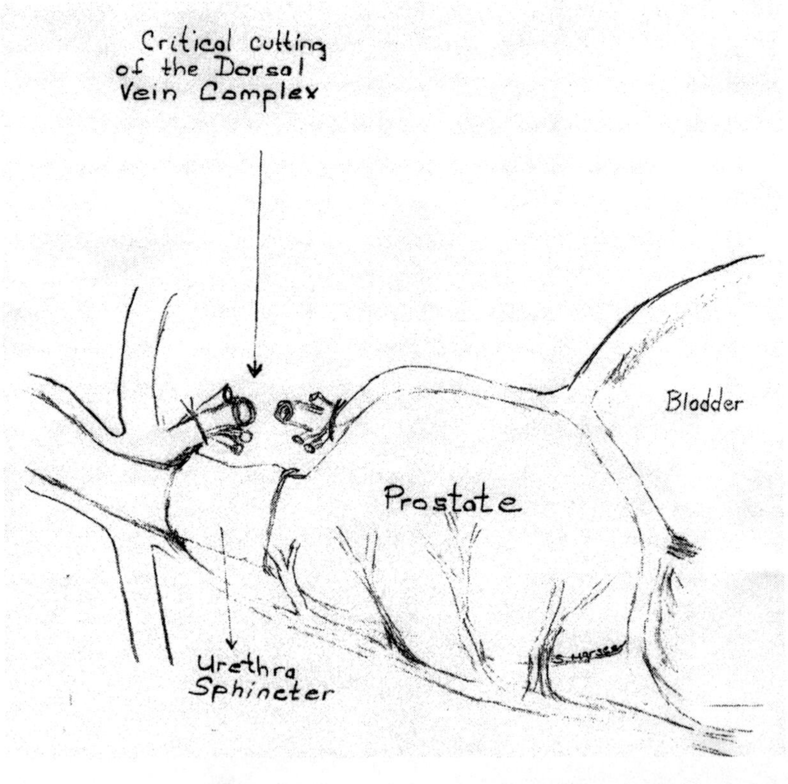

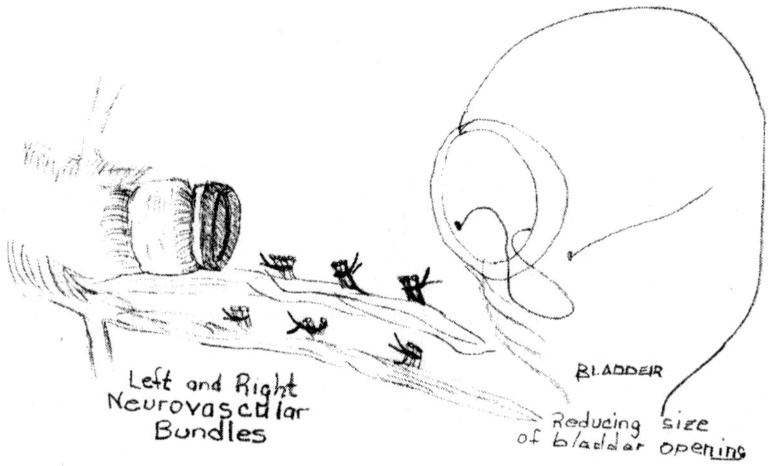

The location for dissecting the urethral sphincter or muscle, away from the prostate is quickly decided upon and the urethra is cut through the Foley catheter while the surgeon hold the catheter upward. If the urethra is cut too close to the prostate some cancer cells might be left behind; but if it is cut to far away from the prostate, the urethral sphincter might be damaged—thus incontinent.

Dr. Badalament then lifts and rotates the prostate from side to side while he separates the prostate from the rectum. Remember, it was via the rectum that Dr. Lee did the ultrasound examination. Then bit by bit the two seminal vesicles, which manufacture and store seminal fluid, are removed together with the prostate.

If nerve sparing is attempted the neurovascular bundles (bundles of nerves that control erection) have been separated from the prostate and tied off. However, they cannot always be saved in which case the result is impotence: (The primary goal here isn't to preserve potency, but to get rid of the nasty cancer.)

Next, the neck of the bladder is opened, and the prostate is dissected away from the muscular wall of the bladder leaving an opening about the size of a quarter.

After the old catheter is removed Dr. Badalament reconfigures the opening in the bladder neck so that its new size matches the urethra. The urethra and bladder are sewn together. Finally a new Foley catheter is inserted through the penis and up through the urethra and into the bladder. To allow for proper healing, the catheter is left in place for approximately three weeks. This allows the urine to flow freely from the body while healing takes place.

Two hours and ten minutes later, another successful Radical Prostatectomy is over without any requirements for blood. (The prostate and the seminal vesicles are sent to the pathologist for further study. In my case the Combination Hormonal Therapy (CHT), had done its job. One cancer had shrunk over fifty-percent and the other, as the Surgical Pathology Report described it, was "indistinguishable from the surrounding tissue." (See Appendices.)

At long last the abdomen is sewed up and the anesthesia equipment is shut down and removed from my body. Now it was to the recovery room and wait for curtain call. With the epidural still in place, the pain should have been minimal, if any.

Was I in for one big surprise?

When I awoke, on a scale of one to ten, the pain was a twenty-five. The epidural was not working.

I felt like someone was holding a hot iron into the fresh wounds.

I was in Hurt City, big time.

And I let everyone on the recovery room floor know it.

A shot of morphine was immediately injected into my body while the anesthesiologist worked to reposition the epidural. The epidural delivers the narcotics based on a scale of one to twelve. With the morphine in me and the epidural repositioned, the mechanism controlling the delivery of the narcotic was set on one, with twelve being the maximum

Both narcotics relieved the pain but every time I dozed off, I stop breathing.

This is not something you want to happen in the recovery room.

A nurse keeping vigil kept awakening me and asking me to breathe.

Approximately four hours later I was taken to the ICU where my family had gathered and waited my arrival. Only this time when they got me up to walk, I couldn't.

I had to sit.

That was all I remembered.

I stopped breathing, again.

One of the male nurses instinctively "kissed me" a couple of times (breathed into me) and thumped my chest. Sharon, our son Kevin and his wife Karen were quickly ushered out of the room.

A nurse kept them company.

I woke up back on the bed breathing pure oxygen with lots of bodies above me saying, "Bruce breathe. Breathe Bruce."

I never did see that tunnel, the bright light or even hear someone call my name.

And I did not experience being on the wall and watching what was going on down below.

Time was non-existent.

I had been completely out, but evidently it was not my time to go. God did not call me home.

After this incident everything was fine until around 1:30am the next morning. With the morphine worn off and the epidural set to one, once again I was in Hurt City. This time on a scale of one to ten, it was a six, maybe seven. Who knows when you are in that much pain?

Fortunately, Sharon had spent the night and was resting with her head on my bed. After complaining several times to the nurses, who had a slight problem understanding the English language, she finally got through to her that the epidural was set too low. Sixty minutes later and after a series of call to the anesthesiologist the epidural was reset to an eight. This setting relieved most of the pain and I was able to get some much-needed rest.

Wednesday morning I was visited by the anesthesiologist who agreed I had been through more pain than was necessary. After a short conversation and prior to leaving my room, he turned the epidural up to its maximum of twelve.

Now I had no pain at all, but a heck of a lot of itching.

Finally it was agreed that we would leave the epidural on eleven. It stayed on eleven until it was removed four days later.

Five days after being admitted to the hospital the external staples were removed from the incision. After Dr. Badalament removed the staples he took hold of the drainage tube, told me to relax and started extracting it out of my abdomen. The sensation was weird, like a gut being pulled from my stomach.

After six long days, I was finally discharged and Sharon drove me to our lake home for continued recuperation. Stopping on the way for a much needed cup of coffee.

I could not believe the extreme to which she had gone to make me comfortable. She had purchased larger clothing, including slacks I could wear over the catheter. The bed, with stacks of pillows, was arranged allowing me to sleep more comfortably. Pads were laid where I usually sit, and reading material was at my disposal. Later our son Kevin brought more reading material including Tom Brokaw's, "The Greatest Generation."

While words cannot express the gratitude one feels when surrounded with love and care such as this, there were times that I was on my worst behavior. The catheter continued to cause me problems and pain. When this occurred I wanted to be alone, I did not want any visitors. I wanted to be left to myself and scream in agony. One particular incident I went to the extreme of calling Dr. Badalament and asked for the "sucker" to be taken out. He agreed to remove the catheter if I insisted. Fortunately my brain knew better then to have it removed with so little time left. I stuck it out.

Eighteen days from surgery, the catheter was finally removed. And when Tracy removed it, as the urine was flowing she told me to stand, then asked me to stop in mid stream. And finally she said, "you won't have any problem."

The Kegels had done the job.

To this date, I have experienced no incontinence whatsoever, not even a drip, and Sharon said removing the catheter alone made me look twenty years younger. (While I had gained weight caused by CHT, I lost fifteen pounds while in the hospital.) Any pain and discomfort that I did experience was caused either by the improper placement of the epidural or that darn catheter.

In fact, bladder spasms caused by the catheter nearly make you want to climb the wall. The ball of my left foot was sore from trying to climb the wall during several of those spasms.

A small amount of discomfort was caused by the scrotum being swollen the size of a softball, but after a couple of weeks it returned to its normal size. Something I was later told that is a natural occurrence after a Radical Prostatectomy. But something I was not informed of prior to surgery.

Once recovery began, walking was not only necessary to prevent blood clotting, it was mandatory.

But the stairs were a no-no.

It was only after three weeks that I was able to visit my computer and to work on my articles. Sharon kindly helped me with all the filing I had to catch-up-on.

Finally it was one day at a time, and each day was better.

Better because you can walk without a catheter running down your thigh to the bag taped to your leg. (Or in my case two bags, I merely connected them together giving me twice the storage for urine. I was even known to have Sharon stop the car while I placed my right leg out the door, flipped open the bottom spout and empty the bags.)

Better because you do not leak or have to wear adults Depends.

Better because you can bathe and dress yourself.

Better because you can change positions in bed at night.

Better because you are not lying in a hospital bed where it is evident that good nursing care must be hard to find.

Better because you have rid yourself of the medication you have been taking for the past six months, and the disgusting cancer is not longer in your body.

But the best is—God is true to His word. He will never leave you or forsake you. Once again God had come through.

IN RETROSPECT—SEVEN MONTHS LATER

It has been a little over seven months now since I was diagnosed with prostate cancer.

Seven months of an unpredictable medical journey for our family.

Seven months a victim of cancer, the silent killer.

Seven months families can do without.

Seven months of no return.

And, seven months of expensive that the insurance company and I could have done without.

It was estimated by the National Cancer Institute that in the United States 218,890 males would be diagnosed with prostate cancer in 2007 and 27,050 would die of it. In the state of Michigan alone, over 6,000 men would be diagnosed with prostate cancer. Approximately 1,000 of these diagnoses came too late.

The incidence of prostate cancer increases with age; and more than 75% of all prostate cancers are diagnosed in men over age 65. For African Americans the incidents are even higher. If anyone has obtained anything out of this book, I hope it is that you will start or continue to have your annual PSA examine. If you are over forty and not scheduling it—start now because very little in research dollars is being allocated to eliminate this disease. In fact, 1997 statistics show that for every AIDS death $66,000 had been spent on research. For each death from prostate cancer, you guessed it; only $452 had been spent on research.

This is worth repeating: you cannot afford to sit by and be a passive patient; you must take an active part in your own health care. At the very least know your PSA level and monitor its elevation. Or do as I did and chart it. In today's world and with a computer it is quite easy.

If I had it to do over knowing what I know now, would I do anything different? Yes, I would make sure the cancer was detected earlier. I would also seek out the same urologist, Dr. Robert Badalament of Rochester, Michigan whom I consider an excellent surgeon, and with whom I have developed a good relationship.

As to the epidural, I consider it a must, but it would be positioned correctly the first time.

I would unquestionably again prepare myself spiritually, physically and psychologically. A regimen of exercise to build up muscle mass is worth all the effort. Since a patient can lose up to five units of blood during a Radical Prostatectomy, a daily intake of 320 mg of slow releasing iron tablets would once more be included in my daily diet.

Again, vitamins E, C and flaxseed would also be included. And to improve my chances of being continent, I would certainly repeat the Kegels, exercising the urethral sphincter muscle at the base of the prostate. This is the muscle that keeps the urine inside the bladder. It can be exercised by stopping the urine in mid stream or by flexing the muscle while sitting or walking. It can even be exercised while driving a car. (After surgery it is located at the base of the bladder.)

While all of this preparation was to pay big dividends post surgery I did have times of complete exhaustion. Walking into a large shopping area with Sharon, all of a sudden I just could not take another step. I told Sharon I would not be able to accompany her any further and returned to the car and waited for her. Lack of testosterone. It would be over a year before it would return to its pre-surgery level.

The hospital?

Well, that is another question worth considering: While I was in the recovery room, in pain and ceasing to breathe every time I dozed off, some nurses were complaining relative to their hours and pay checks loud enough for me to hear when I was awake.

Not very professional.

Later, in a private room, consider this: A diuretic to rid my body of some of the excess fluid was prescribed for me fourteen hours apart. Had I not been listening to Dr. Badalament I would have received it two hours apart.

Fortunately I spoke up.

Otherwise, the medication would have drained me completely dry, or at least it would have felt like it. And in another incident, pain medication was injected into my IV instead of into my buttocks, where it was supposed to have been injected.

And during my hospital stay, I accidentally dropped a pillow and could not pick it up. When a nurse's aide came in, she just walked around it and left the room. It stayed on the floor until I asked someone to pick it up. And on response time: one morning after I rang the nurse's station, ninety minutes later someone showed up, but only after Dr. Badalament brought it to their attention.

This was not the nursing care that I experienced in the 1970's or I expected in the 1990's. Most individuals that I have spoken with, who had a hospital stay in a variety of hospitals, had a like experience. In today's world where the bottom line rules, hospitals are greatly under staffed and many have to resort to nurses from contract firms. Consequently, there is not much loyalty to the hospital or the patient. While the parting words of a nurse were, "Your bag is full, you had better empty it". Within my six day stay, there were some very good nurses and a couple of excellent nurse's aides. In fact one came in while my wife was visiting with me and I was completely out of control with tears flowing freely down my face. The three of us knew the problem; certain medication equals loss of testosterone in my case. Being a male he understood what was happening and acted accordingly.

While I do not mean to pick on the hospitals, we do have a major flaw in our medical system. According to former surgeon Dr. Lucian L. Leape of the Harvard School of Public Health in the December 1994 *Journal of the American Medical Association* (*JAMA*), 180,000 hospitalized Americans can die each year because of errors made by hospital personnel.

A sobering thought while one is lying in their hospital bed. And I seriously doubt if these numbers have changed any. They may have increased.

Regardless of the nursing care, I consider the operation to be successful. Successful because Sharon and I had turned it over to God and He was in control. Successful because of

Dr. Badalament's knowledge and experience, and the final pathology report which came back very favorable. In addition, the six months on Combination Hormonal Therapy (CHT) had done its job. One cancer had shrunk over fifty-percent, and the other, as the lab report described it, was "indistinguishable from the surrounding tissue." Additionally the vas deferens and seminal vesicles were found to be cancer free. Presumably, the bladder neck was also free of cancer.

All this means is I have no medication to take nor did I have to submit myself to Radiation. Fortunately the cancer was caught at a very early stage when my PSA level was 3.2. For the next five years, my PSA would be monitored every six months.

Not only was the operation successful because of Dr. Badalament's expertise, but it was also successful because prayers on my behalf were being offered from Florida, Michigan, North Carolina and Virginia. Our daughter-in-law from Indiana said she would pray for the surgeon's hands.

With this much intercession the surgery had to be a success.

And finally, when the question comes up, "Would you do it again?" the answer is not that simple. If this Radical Prostatectomy has not added at least five years to my life, then the answer is, No.

But on the other hand, Dr. Badalament says with the clean pathology report statistically I can count myself in a group that can expect to have a greater life span. So—of course it was worth it.

After seven months a cancer victim, now I am a cancer survivor.

Any way you look at it, if the radical prostatectomy provides me some more good years with Sharon—that alone will be worth all the pain and agony.

YEAR 2000

December 16, 1998, Doctor Fred Lee of Crittenton Hospital in Rochester, Michigan caringly informed me by telephone that I had Prostate Cancer (PC), the silent killer. In fact, there were two cancers, one in each prostate node.

Under the watchful eyes and skillful hands of Doctor Lee I had underwent an ultrasound with colorflow Doppler the previous day. Later, after the phone conversation with Dr. Lee, I was to learn that I was one of 244,000 adult males in the United States and one of 8,000 in the state of Michigan that was diagnosed in 1998 with PC.

I considered myself somewhat lucky because my PC was detected early. I say somewhat for since age forty I have had an annual PSA examine. So it was not all luck; I do try to take care of myself. Plus I am a child of the King. His blood flows in my veins.

Today more than 27,000 males in the United States are not that lucky; death comes early because the disease was not detected soon enough. The irony is that nine out of ten of these deaths could have been prevented if only they had their annual PSA exam and questioned the doctor relative to the numbers. And understand what the numbers mean. When the numbers start to show a trend, especially upward, seek consultation. Remember, numbers higher than 4.0 could mean the probability for cancer. Some clinics and hospitals will perform the exam for a mere $10, and some free.

PSA or *Prosthetic Specific Antigen* is an enzyme created by the prostate. The *Antigen* is also a soluble toxin. These toxins are normally carried away by the Lymph Node system and eliminated from the body as waste. However, an elevation of the PSA in the blood stream indicates that an abnormal cell condition is present. An elevation of the PSA in the blood may also signal prostate cancer. Likewise the PSA can be elevated with no indication of cancer. Furthermore the PSA can also be low with cancer. (As in my case.)

I had always understood the normal range for one's PSA to be 0.0-4.0 and my PSA had always fallen within the range. However; my PSA in 1996 indicated a value of 1.9, and had risen to 3.2 by 1998. A closer look at the numbers showed an upward trend, a trend I became concerned with. In other words, it was almost doubling every two years.

Once the diagnosis was made, surgeon and urologist Dr. Robert Badalament of Crittenton hospital started me on a regiment of Combination Hormonal Therapy (CHT), the first and mandatory treatment regardless of the initial stage of the disease. The object of CHT was to shrink the PC by fifty-percent prior to freezing or surgical removal of the cancers. As with most therapy's, there are certain side effects. In the case of CHT it was hot flashes, weight gain, fatigue, loss of muscle mass and libido. I found the hot flashes could be controlled with soy products while vitamins and exercise help with the other side effects.

Since deciding on and undergoing a Radical Prostatectomy (a surgical procedure to biopsy the lymph nodes, remove the prostate organ, seminal vesicles, and vas deferens) by Dr. Robert Badalament on July 6, 1999 I consider the recovery to have been excellent.

The six months on CHT had done its job. One of the cancers had shrunk over fifty-percent, and the other, as the lab report described it, was "indistinguishable from the surrounding tissue." (See Appendices.) Additionally the vas deferens, seminal vesicles and bladder neck were found to be cancer free.

I take no medication and underwent no Radiation.

My three-month check-up showed the PSA to be less than point one and the testosterone 112. The average male's testosterone is between 224 and 800. In addition, it will be another four to nine years before I am certain that I am cancer free.

It was to be another twelve to eighteen months before the testosterone level would be revealed in my beard and libido. Most men, or women for that matter, do not fully understand how the sex organs really function and the relationship with the libido. Moreover that erections and orgasms are mutual exclusive. In other words there can be an erection without ever achieving orgasm—or an orgasm can be achieved without ever having an erection. This has created a demand for a product called a ***penile implant*** for those males who cannot achieve an erection after surgery but who continue to enjoy sex.

In fact there are a variety of penile designs that can be implanted by an urologist. However, they can also be very expensive and are not one hundred percent fault free.

During the past year, Sharon and I have been attending one of the many cancer support groups where we continue to hear physicians discuss a variety of ways to treat PC. The controversy over the treatment for PC will continue until the disease is eradicated. Yet, when an individual is diagnosed with PC he can no longer afford to sit-by and be a passive patient.

He must take control of his life and not allow the medical profession or the insurance companies to dictate his future quality of life. PC should not be taken lightly, and no one should rush into any treatment option. In most cases, time is not of the essence.

Obtaining a second and even a third opinion should always be a consideration. There is plenty of information relative to PC; however, one must make a concerted effort to locate it.

It will not come to you.

If you are over forty and have not been scheduling a PSA exam—start now.

This is worth repeating: you cannot afford to sit by and be a passive patient, for you and your family's interest you must take an active part in your own health care. At the very least know your PSA level and monitor its elevation. In other words, do not rely on the physician to tell you it is OK. Ask for your PSA number on paper and maintain a record for your own confort.

NEW TECHNOLOGY

What in the world are those? I asked Dr. Delap as he was explaining the X-ray of my spine to Sharon and I. (See Appendices.) It appears that your Surgeon was handy with the stapler he replied. Then he explained that the titanium staples were placed in my abdomen during surgery. He further clarified that the two staples in form of an X was where the Dorsal Venus Complex, a large group of veins had been tied off. I inquired as to how long the staples would be there. Should your body be exhumed five thousand years after you are buried they will be there, Dr. Delap replied. Well I don't think so I retorted I am to be cremated. It is really Sharon who wants to be cremated; her ashes mixed with paint and then the ceiling of my bedroom painted. She plans to keep an eye on me. So she informs me.

Most patients who undergo surgery are rarely informed of what is left behind in their bodies and for those who do have a look-see it is only by the way of an X-ray. However, with the newer much improved techniques for removing the cancerous prostate the chance for something being left behind or lots of staples, as in my case, is becoming rare.

Until recently, patient's treatment for localized prostate cancer included Radical Prostatectomy, Radiation or Cryosurgery. Unfortunately, sometimes these treatments are associated with significant side effects including impotence and incontinence of urine.

The Radical Prostatectomy, a surgical approach, requires the complete removal of the prostate including the seminal vesicles, deferent canals, and part of the bladder neck. The radical is performed under general anesthesia and requires hospitalization from three to five days and another six weeks of healing.

Laparoscopy (pronounced "lap-a-ROSS-coe-pee") is another surgical procedure that is performed through very small incisions in the abdomen. According to www.ehealthMD.com web site Laparoscopy uses a pencil-thin instrument called a laparoscope giving the surgeon an exceptionally clear view, on a TV monitor, of the inside of the abdominal cavity. Again this type of surgery is called "minimally invasive" because of the very small incisions that are made. More information on this procedure may also be found at www.ehealthMD.com.

On the other hand, External Beam Radiotherapy (EBRT) treatment is a non-invasive technique requiring high levels of Radiation. These treatments are completed in a cancer center over a 7-week period for a total of 35 treatments. Complications can include fatigue and malaise while long-term side effects may include erectile dysfunction and incontinence. It is said that EBRT is associated with a 70% increased risk of rectal cancer.

An additional treatment option for PC includes High Dose Rate (HDR) Brachytherapy, a surgical procedure during which radioactive pellets are inserted into the cancerous prostate organ by way of the perineum. The area between the scrotum and the rectum. HDR is said to be applicable to virtually all stages of localized prostate cancer and many other types of cancer as well.

Cryosurgery is where small probes are surgically placed into the prostate and the cancerous areas are frozen thus destroying portions of prostate tissue. This too is by way of the perineum. Each procedure carries with it their own significant side effects.

While some of the older technology continues to be performed on PC patients some of these newer techniques are now available. Take for example a radio commercial heard throughout southern Michigan. Saint Joseph Mercy Hospital of Ann Arbor, Michigan promotes the CyberKnife as a new revolutionary technology to treat tumors that were once considered inoperable. The hospitals web site states that the CyberKnife uses the latest robotic radiosurgery, which combines image guidance technology and computer controlled robotics.

The site goes on to state, with this type of pinpoint accuracy, our skilled physicians are now able to treat areas of the body, such as the spine, lung, prostate, liver and pancreas. And because it's non-invasive, treatment can be delivered in a single or multiple visits, at the patient's convenience.

Central Baptist Hospital in Lexington, Kentucky had this additional information in one of their advertisement: Despite its name, the CyberKnife is a highly advanced outpatient procedure that offers many cancer patients better results, high comfort and hope. It uses X-ray-image cameras and computer technology similar to that used to guide missiles. With sub-millimeter accuracy, the CyberKnife provides an alternative to traditional surgery without the incision, blood, anesthesia or associated pain.

Rapid technical advances in miniaturize surgical tools, fiber optics and miniature video systems enables new developments in minimally invasive surgery. What this means for patients in some cases, is no incisions or pain and minimal side effects. In a world of high tech a variety of new weapons are now in the surgeons arsenal they did not have years ago. Many are now proven and at the surgeons disposal for battling PC.

An individual that I have known for some time tells me that when he was diagnosed with PC he chose to have the Robotic Prostatectomy Operation at Henry Ford Hospital in Detroit, Michigan. Surgeons at Henry Ford Hospital's Vattikuti Urology Institute developed the technique of nerve-sparing robotic prostatectomy—the Veil of Aphrodite—that results in significantly better erectile function, so states their material. In their literature the Institute states that thousands of patients from around the world have come to the Vattikuti Institute for their prostatectomy surgery.

They further assert, the procedure not only removes the cancer, but also has a high probability of preserving sexual function and urinary control. And again this procedure is completed with minimal side effects and leaves very small scars. While my stay was five days in the hospital this friend said he was out in three. Quite an advancement, I would say.

The newest technique and in the experimental stage appears to be a treatment that is just the opposite of Cryosurgery and currently available only in Canada. Instead of freezing the cancerous tumors this technique applies heat. Ablatherm (HIFU) is a non-invasive and highly precise procedure using high intensity focused ultrasound. During the procedure an Ablatherm probe is placed into the rectum after administration of anesthesia. A high intensity and focused beam of ultrasound is directed into the prostate, which rapidly raises the temperature of the prostate to 85 degrees Celsius and destroys the prostate tissue. The procedure is completed without blood loss or exposure to Radiation. HIFU materials also states that the procedure can be used on patients with localized PC (clinical stage T-1 or T-2) who would otherwise be considered curable only by Radiation or a Radical Prostatectomy.

Keep in mind however; as with any new technology don't be the first person on the block to test the new procedure. And if possible do not agree to be the test Guinea Pig because marketing techniques can get ahead of the science.

Although minimally invasive robotic surgery may eventually offer advantages over traditional surgery for all men, there is a learning curve among surgeons for using the technology, said Dr. Jim Hu, the lead author of a study published October 13, 2009 in the Journal of the American Medical Association (AMA). The study noted details that men should know about: The most serious complications—including incontinence and erectile dysfunction—appeared more often in men who underwent minimally invasive surgery compared to traditional surgery. However, those who underwent the minimally invasive surgery also experienced more urinary—and genital-function complication; 4.7 percent compared to 2.1 percent who underwent traditional surgery.

Chuck a good friend of Sharon and I was informed approximately eight years ago that he had PC. That was during the time that he and I first met. While I in no uncertain terms have any medical experience, when Chuck informed me of the diagnosis I suggested that with his age and health he do nothing but watchful-waiting. Chuck is now ninety-two. He continues to undergo CHT and has his ups and downs.

When Chuck's PSA reaches the threshold he is given an injection and monitored. After the PSA declines, over a period of time it will once again start to increase. Chuck's knows that this will continue for the remainder of his life. He is thankful to be alive. Thankful that he can attend church weekly, and thankful that he can continue to work in his vegetable garden.

CONTROVERSY & INFORMATION

There continues to be a great deal of controversy surrounding the treatment of Prostate Cancer (PC). In recent months and years treating PC has made the major television networks, the radio talk shows (one of which I participated in) and comments from the American Cancer Society (ACS).

However, Dr. Robert Leibowitz of the Compassionate Oncology Medical Group in California is very assertive in his video titled, "Emerging Concepts and Management of all Stages of Prostate Cancer." Leibowitz considers PC systemic; therefore it should be treated as such. Prescribing a thirteen-month triple dose of Combination Hormonal Therapy (CHT), the first and mandatory treatment regardless of the initial stage of the disease, for localized PC (confined to the prostate) Leibowitz claims a 100% cure rate. While some individuals may think Leibowitz to be somewhat extreme (considering a triple dose of CHT for thirteen months at a cost of over a thousand dollars per month and the potential side effects) some of his tenets make sense and the video is worth watching. In fact, prior to my surgery I delivered a copy to my urologist for his review and comments. (The video may be purchased by calling (310) 229-3555. A partial refund is given when the tape is returned.)

Dr. Fred Lee, Director of the Crittenton Prostate Center in Rochester, Michigan and a recipient of the 1999 International College of Surgeons "Honorary Fellowship," claims eighty to ninety percent success with his Cryosurgery. (Cryosurgery is a freezing technique using ultrasound as a guide to provide detailed images allowing safe and precise freezing of the prostate.) However, Cryosurgery is not for everyone, the same way the Radical Prostatectomy, Radiation or seed implant (SI) is not for everyone. The impotency rate for Cryosurgery is currently eighty-five percent. Incontinence is four percent for Cryosurgery, thirty-one percent for a Radical Prostatectomy and eleven percent for Radiation.

This is precisely the reason an individual with PC needs to do his homework.

He cannot sit by and be a passive patient.

After all, research is done before a new home or new car is purchased.

I think PC to be a little more important than either of these.

A few years ago there were those in the medical profession who believed that Cryosurgery would eventually replace the Radical Prostatectomy (Gold Standard) as the procedure of choice. In other words, the Radical Prostatectomy will become obsolete. In fact, as of July 1999, Cryosurgery was removed by Medicare as an experimental classification procedure and Medicare began to pay for the treatment. In a support group that I attended, many of those scheduled for Radical Prostatectomy had canceled and opted for Cryosurgery.

Furthermore; recent research as reported in JNCI Journal of the National Cancer Institute (www.jnci.oxfordjournals.

org) and reported on the nightly news, now shows that the learning curve for prostate cancer recurrence after radical prostatectomy was steep and did not start to plateau until a surgeon had completed approximately 250 prior operations. The predicted probabilities of recurrence at 5 years were 17.9% for patients treated by surgeons with 10 prior operations and 10.7% for patients treated by surgeons with 250 prior operations. The conclusion was, as the surgeon's experience increases, cancer control after radical prostatectomy improves, presumably because of improved surgical technique. As you can see, it is very prudent to have questions written on paper to ask your surgeon. I think we can safely say, "There are no dumb questions in this game".

While having my annual colonoscopy, my proctologist Dr. Farouk Tootla informed me that he, too, had undergone a Radical Prostatectomy. In our chitchat prior to the procedure, he was very clear in that he considers Radical Prostatectomy to be the best option, and as a surgeon, he was absolutely against Cryosurgery

"**M**an to Man, Surviving Prostate Cancer," written by the late Michael Korda and published by Random House, is a must read for PC victims and an excellent gift for males of the family. (I give the name "victims" to individuals who have yet to undergo treatment. Survivors are those cured.)

Korda was a survivor of a Radical Prostatectomy and his writing style makes for interesting reading, even if you are not a PC victim. Korda describes in detail the problems he encountered prior to, during his diagnosis, later treatment and recovery. However, Korda had the foresight (and means) to purchase items he would need post surgery, i.e., rubber sheets, adult diapers, sterile gauze and tape. Being a vice president of a major publishing house, Korda's income allowed him the luxury of a part time nurse and a male attendant while recuperating at home. Korda also employed a private plane to take him home from the hospital. (Having corresponded with Korda, he also wrote an interesting letter.) Unfortunately, Korda has since passed away.

Another book worth the purchase is, "Prostate & Cancer, A Family guide to Diagnosis, Treatment & Survival" by Sheldon Marks, published by Fisher Books. Marks, an urologist, has taken various questions he has been asked during his years of practice, organizes them in book form and supplies the answers. Marks concludes his book with a final chapter on death, but caution the reader prior to reading the last chapter.

"The Prostate A Guide For The Men And The Women Who Love Them" by Janet Farrar Worthington", published by Warner Books is the most biased reading material, promoting the Radical Prostatectomy, that I have read. The book in effect promotes Dr. Patrick C. Walsh, who pioneered the nerve sparing procedure and Director of Urology at Johns Hopkins University School of Medicine. While the author did present some excellent information relative to how PC is stimulated and controlled, she focused too much, I felt, on the surgical removal of the prostate.

PAACT, "Patient Advocates for Advanced Cancer Treatment, Inc.," a free quarterly magazine out of Grand Rapids, Michigan (616) 453-1477 is a Cancer Communication Newsletter. The magazine is an excellent source of valuable information for those with PC. It features everything from helpful hints, food recipes, and cryosurgical reports to upcoming symposiums and vitamin sources. PAACT Web Page is located at www.paactusa.org.

The magazine "PCRI Insight" published by The Prostate Cancer Research Institute out of Marina Del Rey, California focuses more on the current research relative to PC and the new developments in Prostate Cancer treatment. Again, this is free literature with their Web Page at: www.pcri.org.

Information for almost all major medication can be found on the Internet. By typing in www, dot, and then the name of the medication followed by the dot com. you will be taken to the site. An example would be www.casodex.com. A host of information relative to the pharmaceutical firm and important data will be listed.

You can rest assured that once you have completed your PC treatment be it Radiation, Radical Prostatectomy, Cryosurgery or some newer technique you will be invited to a local support group. All groups welcome spouses or significant others.

Relationships and friendships can often change. Unfortunately, a stigma is sometimes attached to cancer by those who are uninformed or do not take the time to learn about the disease.

The controversy over PC will continue until the disease is eradicated. If not on this earth then certainly when Christ sets up His kingdom. Yet, when an individual is diagnosed with PC he can no longer afford to sit-by and be a passive patient. He must take control of his life and not allow the medical profession or the insurance companies to dictate his future quality of life. PC is not to be taken lightly, and no one should rush into any treatment option.

Obtaining a second and even a third opinion should always be a consideration. Keep in mind that at this moment in your life, time is not of the essence.

It may, in fact it will, consume many hours of praying, seeking God's guidance, reading, researching (including the Internet) discussing, seeking sound information and formulating one's own opinion in order to reach a decision that he and his family must live with for the remainder of his life.

During discussions with those in the medical profession concerning PC, life is spoken of in terms of "five and ten year survival rates." PC is a silent killer, with a war raging inside the victim's body. The body has become a war zone. If total victory is to be the outcome, the war has to be fought with every weapon one has access to in his defense arsenal.

Sooner or later one in six men will be diagnosed with PC. Which of the six will you be?

APPENDICES

PRE SURGERY

Marcee, Bruce

59 yrs.

PSA 1.9 ('96) '97 (2.4) '98 (3.3)

Prognosis Factors

1. Location of CA R & L bases
2. Size of Cancers 2MM (R) (3) - 6MM (L) (9MM)
3. Perineural involvement - negative
4. Gleason score 3+3
6. DNA - Diploid

Treatment Options.

1. RADICAL

J. Natl' Cancer Institute
89 : 1117, 1997
TALCOTT, JA et al — Harvard

Potency
one nerve 17%
two nerve 21%

2. Radiation

3. CRYOSURGERY -
81%

218739006 O

MARSEE, BRUCE E M 03/08/1939 CAN 09/01/1995 08:30

09/01/1995 OP 185 R/O PROSTATE CA

**

US PROSTATE TRANSRECTAL

PROSTATE ULTRASOUND:

Digital rectal examination: Nonspecific

The gland volume is 31 grams.

The predicted PSA is between 2.1 and 3.7 ng/ml.

The patient's PSA level is 1.48 ng/ml.

The ultrasound study revealed very minimal degree of BPH changes. There is no evidence of malignancy.

CONCLUSIONS:

There is only a minimal degree of BPH changes. There is no evidence of malignancy at this time.

DICTATED: 9/1/95
TRANSCRIBED: 9/1/95

218739009 O JEA\ .SH

MARSEE, BRUCE E M 03/08/1939 MA 12/15/1998 11:35

12/15/1998 OP ELEVATED PSA 79093

**

US PROSTATE WITH BIOPSY Dictated by:

PROSTATE ULTRASOUND AND BIOPSY:

SERUM PSA: 3.2 ng/ml

Slow increase in PSA since 1995. Increasing from 1.5 to 1.9 to 2.4 ng/ml and presently at 3.2 ng/ml. In 1995, his gland volume was 31 cc and presently at 35 cc. His predicted PSA is 2.2 ng/ml.

1.2 cm lesion at right mid gland which was sampled as well as any other suspicious regions. No complications from biopsy.

FL/tlk
DICTATED: 12/15/98
TRANSCRIBED: 12/16/98

DO NOT MAIL-HAND DELIVER PROSTATE CTR

CRITTENTON HOSPITAL
SURGICAL PATHOLOGY REPORT

PATIENT: Marsee, Bruce
Medical Record Number: 218739009
Patient Location: RAD

SURGPATH ACCESSION: S98-14374
Birth Date: 03/08/1939 Sex: M
Doctor:

Preoperative diagnosis: R/O CA
Clinical information: PSA 3.2, TRUS RM
Postoperative diagnosis: Same
Specimen source: Prostate: 1) RM x 3 2) RB 3) RA 4) LB 5) LA

Date of procedure: 12/15/98

Date and time in lab: 12/15/98 1246

****** ATTENTION: POSITIVE REPORT ******

DIAGNOSIS:
1, 2, 3, 4, AND 5. PROSTATE GLAND, ULTRASOUND-GUIDED TRANSRECTAL NEEDLE BIOPSIES: ADENOCARCINOMA.

GROSS:
1. In formalin labeled "RM" are three, 1.3, 1.5, and 2.0 cm, blue-tipped tissue cores. In toto, 1 block.

2. In formalin labeled "RB" is a 2.0 cm, blue-tipped tissue core. In toto, 1 block.

3. In formalin labeled "RA" is a 1.1 cm, blue-tipped tissue core. In toto, 1 block.

4. In formalin labeled "LB" is a 1.2 cm, blue-tipped tissue core. In toto, 1 block.

5. In formalin labeled "LA" is a 1.5 cm, blue-tipped tissue core. In toto, 1 block. TB/ih

MICRO:
1, 2, 3, 4, and 5. Microscopic examined.

Malignant locations: Right base and left base.
Benign locations: Right mid, right apex, and left apex.
Gleason grade: 3 + 3 = 6.
Size: Right base 1.5 mm., left base 6 mm.
Extraprostatic invasion: No.
Perineural invasion: No.
Comments: Carcinoma is at or near the inked end of both involved cores.
Ploidy study: Left base biopsy (4) sent.

/ih
12/16/98
SNOP 8143

Special stains: No

Electronically Signed

Internal audit:

cc: Histopath Associates
Prostate Center

HISTOPATHOLOGY ASSOCIATES, INC

PATIENT ID #

DNA PLOIDY ANALYSIS REPORT

SPECIMEN ID# S# 98-08675

PATIENT'S NAME Marsee, Bruce BIRTH DATE 3/8/39 SOC. SEC. NUMBER

SUBMITTING DOCTOR SEX M DATE RECEIVED 12/17/98 DATE REPORTED 12/31/98

CLINICAL DIAGNOSIS:

Crittenton Hospital

Gleason's grade 3 + 3 = 6
Prostate

PERTINENT CLINICAL HISTORY:

PLOIDY
Block IV
Also 1 slide received

SPECIMEN DESCRIPTION:

S98-08675
Submitted is a paraffin block, sectioned at 7 μ and stained by the Feulgen technique for the quantitative labeling of DNA using lot-controlled reagents (CAS™). The staining batch includes a control slide of rat hepatocytes.

TISSUE ADEQUACY:

Review of the Feulgen stained slides indicates:
_X_ sufficient tissue for analysis

ANALYSIS TECHNIQUE:

The Feulgen-stained control and patient slides are quantitatively analyzed for nuclear size and DNA content (using optical density measurements of the staining intensity of individual nuclei). This analysis is performed on directly visualized neoplastic and non-neoplastic cells using the Quantitative DNA Analysis computer program on a CAS 200 Image Analysis System.

RESULTS:

Control Cells:

Number counted (N)	23	(NL: 20)
Coefficient of Variation (CV)	1.60	(NL: 0-4%)
Relative DNA Mass (ΣOD)	7412	(NL: 7200-8900)

Non-neoplastic Cells (Patient):

Number counted (N)	29	
Coefficient of Variation (CV)	3.89	(NL: 0-10%)
Relative DNA Mass (picograms/nucleus)	6.60	(NL: 6.47-7.89)

HISTOPATHOLOG ASSOCIATES, INC

(248) 788-1627 FAX (248) 788-2325

Page 2 of 2

DNA PLOIDY ANALYSIS REPORT

SPECIMEN ID# S# 98-08675

PATIENT'S NAME Marsee, Bruce

RESULTS (cont.)

Neoplastic Cells (Patient):

Total N 156

Peak 1:

N	137
% CV	5.29
Avg. DNA (pg)	6.96
DNA Index*	0.97

Peak 2:

N	18 (S phase)
% CV	
Avg. DNA (pg)	
DNA Index*	

Peak 3:

N	
% CV	
Avg. DNA (pg)	
DNA Index*	

*DNA Index = pg. DNA per nucleus of abnormal cells / pg. DNA per nucleus of normal cells (7.18 pg.)

Patient id : S9808675 MARSEE,BRUCE
Accession #: CILD98842 AC 9.8 PROSTATE
DNA Index based on 7.18 Picograms

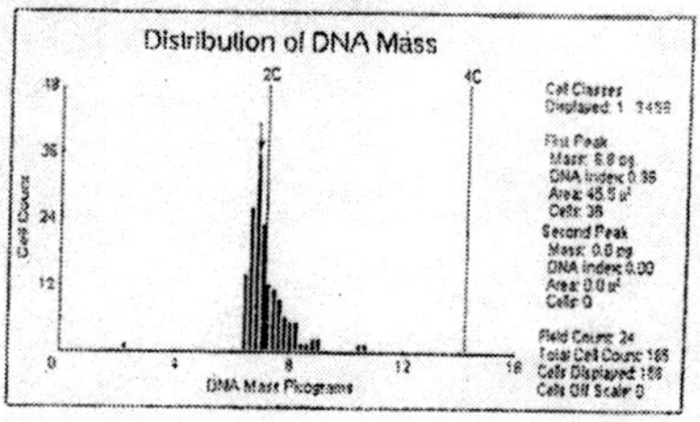

INTERPRETATION AND COMMENTS:

Review of the biopsy reveals an adenocarcinoma of the prostate, Gleason's 3 + 3 = 6 (moderately differentiated). The DNA ploidy histogram shows a dominant diploid peak with proliferative activity estimated at 11%. It should be noted that image analysis of Feulgen stained sections allows only an estimation of the proliferative activity because only 150-250 nuclei are studied. This limited sample is subject to larger statistical variation than are the thousands of nuclei studied by flow cytometry. According to current literature, finding an exclusively diploid tumor cell population with low proliferative activity (less than 15%) indicates this patient has a better prognosis than if the cell population were non-diploid or diploid with high proliferative activity.

77100-81403
CPT 88358 X 1
CPT 88313 X 1
DIPLOID 11% PA
MRA:ss
DT: 12/31/98

DNA ploidy analysis is considered an experimental procedure. Data derived from such analysis should be used only in conjunction with standard clinical and pathologic diagnostic criteria for the management of patient

218739010 O

MARSEE, BRUCE E M 03/08/1939 DKC 12/22/1998 08:15

12/22/1998 OP CA PROSTATE/

**

CHEST 2 VIEWS Dictated by: ,

CHEST:

Frontal and lateral views were compared with 11/23//96. The heart size is normal. A focal infiltrate is not seen in the lungs. The pulmonary vascularity is normal. The costophrenic angles are clear. There is a vague density noted laterally over the right upper lung. It may represent a focal area of pleural thickening. Unfortunately, the previous film was a portable film. Direct comparison is therefore not possible. If the patient has old standard views performed since 1996, they would be very helpful for comparison. If not, a repeat examination with an apical lordotic view is recommended.

KV/mp D: 12/22/98 T: 12/22/98

DO NOT MAIL-HAND DELIVER PROSTATE CTR

218739010 O

MARSEE, BRUCE E M 03/08/1939 DKC 12/22/1998 08:00

12/22/1998 OP CA PROSTATE

CAT ABD & PELVIS W/ CONTRAST Dictated by:

CT SCAN OF ABDOMEN AND PELVIS:

HISTORY PROVIDED: Prostate carcinoma.

TECHNIQUE: Multiple CT axial images are obtained from the dome of the diaphragm through the ischial tuberosities, following the uneventful administration of oral and nonionic intravenous contrast material.

FINDINGS: Limited evaluation of the lung bases demonstrates minimal bibasilar atelectatic changes which are likely positional in nature and of doubtful clinical significance.

In the abdomen, the liver, spleen, adrenal glands, and kidneys have a normal CT appearance. The pancreas also appears normal. The gallbladder is present.

No abdominal or retroperitoneal lymphadenopathy is noted. No ascites is seen. Moderate degenerative changes in the regional musculo-skeletal structures are seen.

Regarding the pelvis, no inguinal or iliac lymphadenopathy is definitely identified. Calcifications are seen within the prostate gland which are not uncommon in the patient's age group. Fat plane between the prostate gland and the obturator internis muscles appears well preserved bilaterally. No free fluid is seen in the pelvis. There is no evidence of ureteral obstruction bilaterally.

IMPRESSION:

No definite evidence of metastatic disease from the patient's reported prostate carcinoma is seen.

PR/sg D: 12/22/98 T: 12/22/98

DO NOT MAIL-HAND DELIVER PROSTATE CTR

218739010 O

MARSEE, BRUCE E M 03/08/1939 SLW 12/22/1998 10:42

I 12/22/1998 OP 185 PROSTATE CA

**

BONE SCAN WHOLE BODY Dictated by:

BONE SCAN:

25.7 millicuries of Technetium MDP are injected. Scintiphotograms are made of the entire skeletal structures.

There is a normal distribution of radionuclides in the skeletal structures. No abnormal localization is shown.

CONCLUSION:

Normal bone scan.

KS/sg D: 12/22/98 T: 12/22/98

DO NOT MAIL-HAND DELIVER PROSTATE CTR

January 12, 1999

RE: MR. BRUCE MARSEE
DATE OF BIRTH: 3/8/39

NOTE FOR CHART:

Mr. Marsee was seen on December 15, 1998, regarding an elevating serum PSA which attained a level of 3.2 ng/ml. His gland volume was 35 grams for a predicted TZ PSA of 2.2 ng/ml. He was found to have an abnormal lesion involving right base, and biopsy of suspicious areas in the remaining gland proved that the right and left base were involved by a gleason 3+3 with no evidence for extracapsular extension. He subsequently was advised to have a bone scan and CT scan which were both negative. He has an appointment to see Dr. Badalament as regards combination hormonal therapy.

A discussion of his case with the patient centered about the fact that his cancer appears to be clinically localized, and he should do well no matter what treatment option he selects.

He was advised to contact PAACT for information regarding prostate cancer and to join man-to-man groups to discuss treatment options.

The use of combination hormonal therapy for a maximum of 3 to 6 months was advised prior to primary treatment.

I did discuss briefly with him cryosurgery which is our specialty and shared the results of no evidence of disease being 81% proven by biopsy. 71% of these patients have PSAs of 0.5 ng/ml or less. These results are equal to or somewhat better than those of either radical surgery or radiation therapy. The risks of the various treatment options were just touched on. I am to have a more in depth review of treatment options with him in early January.

DICTATED: 01/11/99
TRANSCRIBED: 01/12/99

POST SURGERY

Com ation of PSA, Clinical Stage, and Gleason Scor Predict Pathological Stage of Localized Prosta ancer

Partin AW and associates: Journal of Ame... n Medical Association, 277:1445-1451. 1997

Table 5.—Prediction of Organ-Confined Disease, Established Capsular Penetration, Seminal Vesicle Involvement, and Lymph Nodal Involvement*

Gleason Score	PSA, 0.0-4.0 ng/mL, Clinical Stage T1a	T1b	T1c	T2a	T2b	T2c	T3a	PSA, 4.1-10.0 ng/mL, Clinical Stage T1a	T1b	T1c	T2a	T2b	T2c	T3a
Organ-Confined Disease														
2-4	90 (84-95)	80 (72-86)	89 (86-92)	81 (75-86)	72 (65-79)	77 (69-83)	...	84 (75-92)	70 (60-79)	83 (78-88)	71 (64-78)	61 (52-69)	66 (57-74)	43 (27-58)
5	82 (73-90)	66 (57-73)	81 (76-84)	68 (63-72)	57 (50-62)	62 (55-69)	40 (26-53)	72 (60-85)	53 (44-63)	71 (67-75)	55 (51-60)	43 (38-49)	49 (42-55)	27 (17-39)
6	78 (68-88)	61 (52-69)	78 (74-81)	64 (59-68)	52 (46-57)	57 (51-64)	35 (22-48)	67 (55-82)	47 (38-57)	67 (64-70)	51 (47-54)	38 (34-43)	43 (38-49)	23 (14-34)
7		43 (34-53)	63 (56-68)	47 (41-52)	34 (29-39)	38 (32-45)	19 (11-29)	49 (34-68)	29 (21-38)	49 (45-54)	33 (29-38)	22 (18-26)	25 (20-30)	11 (6-17)
8-10		31 (20-43)	52 (41-62)	36 (27-45)	24 (17-32)	27 (18-36)	...	35 (18-62)	18 (11-28)	37 (28-46)	23 (16-31)	14 (9-19)	15 (10-22)	6 (3-10)
Established Capsular Penetration														
2-4	9 (4-15)	19 (13-26)	10 (7-14)	18 (13-23)	25 (19-32)	21 (14-28)	...	14 (7-23)	27 (18-37)	15 (11-20)	26 (19-33)	35 (26-43)	29 (21-37)	44 (30-59)
5	17 (9-26)	32 (24-40)	18 (15-22)	30 (26-35)	40 (34-46)	34 (27-40)	51 (38-65)	25 (14-36)	42 (32-51)	27 (23-30)	41 (36-46)	50 (45-55)	43 (37-50)	57 (46-68)
6	19 (11-29)	35 (27-43)	21 (18-25)	34 (30-38)	43 (38-48)	37 (31-43)	53 (41-65)	27 (15-39)	44 (35-53)	30 (27-33)	44 (41-48)	52 (48-56)	46 (40-51)	57 (47-67)
7		44 (35-54)	31 (26-36)	45 (40-50)	51 (46-57)	45 (38-52)	52 (40-63)	36 (20-51)	48 (36-60)	40 (35-44)	52 (48-57)	54 (49-59)	48 (42-54)	48 (37-58)
8-10		43 (32-56)	34 (27-44)	47 (38-56)	48 (40-57)	42 (33-52)	...	34 (17-58)	42 (28-57)	40 (33-49)	49 (42-57)	46 (39-53)	40 (31-48)	34 (24-46)
Seminal Vesicle Involvement														
2-4	0 (0-2)	1 (0-3)	1 (0-1)	1 (0-2)	2 (1-5)	2 (1-5)	...	1 (0-4)	2 (0-6)	1 (0-3)	2 (1-5)	4 (1-9)	5 (1-10)	10 (3-23)
5	1 (0-3)	2 (0-4)	1 (1-2)	2 (1-3)	3 (2-4)	3 (2-6)	7 (3-14)	2 (0-5)	3 (1-7)	2 (1-3)	3 (2-5)	5 (3-8)	6 (4-10)	12 (6-20)
6	1 (0-3)	2 (0-4)	1 (1-2)	2 (1-3)	3 (2-4)	4 (2-5)	7 (4-13)	2 (0-6)	3 (1-6)	2 (2-3)	3 (2-4)	5 (4-7)	6 (4-9)	11 (6-18)
7	...	6 (1-13)	4 (2-7)	6 (4-8)	10 (6-14)	12 (7-17)	19 (10-31)	6 (0-19)	9 (2-18)	8 (5-11)	10 (8-13)	15 (11-19)	18 (13-24)	26 (17-36)
8-10		11 (2-23)	9 (5-16)	12 (7-19)	17 (11-25)	21 (12-31)	...	10 (0-34)	15 (4-29)	15 (10-22)	19 (13-26)	24 (17-31)	28 (20-37)	35 (23-48)
Lymph Node Involvement														
2-4	0 (0-1)	0 (0-1)	0 (0-0)	0 (0-0)	0 (0-1)	0 (0-1)	...	0 (0-2)	1 (0-3)	0 (0-1)	0 (0-1)	1 (0-2)	1 (0-2)	1 (0-5)
5	0 (0-2)	1 (0-2)	0 (0-0)	0 (0-1)	1 (0-2)	1 (0-2)	2 (0-4)	1 (0-5)	2 (1-5)	0 (0-1)	1 (0-1)	2 (1-3)	2 (1-3)	3 (1-7)
6	1 (0-7)	2 (1-5)	0 (0-1)	1 (0-1)	2 (1-3)	2 (1-4)	5 (2-9)	3 (0-15)	5 (2-11)	1 (1-2)	2 (1-3)	4 (3-6)	4 (3-6)	9 (5-15)
7		6 (2-13)	1 (1-3)	2 (1-4)	5 (2-8)	5 (2-9)	9 (4-17)	8 (0-32)	12 (5-23)	3 (2-5)	4 (3-6)	9 (6-12)	9 (6-13)	15 (8-23)
8-10	...	14 (5-27)	4 (2-7)	5 (2-9)	10 (5-17)	10 (4-18)	...	18 (0-55)	23 (10-43)	8 (4-12)	9 (5-13)	16 (11-24)	17 (10-26)	24 (13-38)

*Numbers represent percent predictive probability (95% confidence interval). Ellipses indicate lack of sufficient data to calculate probability. PSA indicates prostate-specific antigen.

My Clinical Stage is: T1c
My PSA is: 5.2
My Gleason Score is: 6

My chance of having cancer confined to my prostate following radical prostatectomy is : 78
My chance of having prostate outside my prostate following radical prostatectomy is: 21
My chance of having cancer into the seminal vesicles is: 1
My chance of having spread of my cancer into my lymph nodes is: 0

Rochester Urology, P.C., Robert A. Badalament, M.D., 248-650-4699

Calculation Results http://rattler.cameron.edu/cgi-bin/partin1

The Partin Numbers

Base Data

PSA: 3.2
Gleason: 6
Clinical Staging: T1C

Predictions

- Organ contained disease: 69 %
- Capsular Penetration: 34 %
- Seminal Vesicle Invasion: 1 %
- Lymph Node Invasion: 2 %

CRITTENTON HOSPITAL
SURGICAL PATHOLOGY REPORT

PATIENT: Marsee, Bruce
Medical Record Number:
Patient Location: 731A

SURGPATH ACCESSION: S99-7780
Birth Date: 03/08/1939 Sex: M
Doctor: Robert Badalament, M.D.

Preoperative diagnosis: Prostate cancer
Clinical information: Prostate cancer and hormone therapy
Postoperative diagnosis: Same
Specimen source: 1. Right pelvic lymph node, 2. Right vas deferens, 3. Left vas deferens, 4. Left pelvic lymph node, 5. Right pelvic lymph node, 6. Prostate gland

Date of procedure: 07/06/99

Date and time in lab: 07/06/99 1246

******** ATTENTION: POSITIVE REPORT ********

DIAGNOSIS:
1. RIGHT PELVIC LYMPH NODE: ONE LYMPH NODE FREE OF TUMOR.
2 AND 3. BILATERAL SEGMENTS OF VAS DEFERENS: FREE OF TUMOR.
4. LEFT PELVIC LYMPH NODES: TWO LYMPH NODES FREE OF TUMOR.
5. RIGHT PELVIC LYMPH NODES: TWO LYMPH NODES FREE OF TUMOR.
6. PROSTATE GLAND: ADENOCARCINOMA.

GROSS:
1. Received fresh labeled "right pelvic lymph node" is a 2.0 x 1.5 x 0.8 cm lymph node surrounded by a small amount of adipose tissue. A representative section is submitted for frozen section. The remaining portion of lymph node is submitted, one block.

FROZEN SECTION DIAGNOSIS (one block): Lymph node free of tumor. MRV/elm

2. Received in formalin labeled "right vas" is a 3.0 x 0.2 cm cylindrical structure. Serially sectioned and totally submitted, one block.

3. Received in formalin labeled "left vas" is a 3.0 x 0.2 cm diameter cylindrical structure. Serially sectioned and totally submitted, one block. MRV/elm

4. Received fresh labeled "left pelvic lymph nodes" are two lymph nodes, each of which is approximately 1.0 cm greatest dimension, surrounded by adipose tissue. The nodes are totally submitted for frozen section.

FROZEN SECTION DIAGNOSIS (one block): Two lymph nodes free of tumor. MRV/elm

5. Received fresh labeled "right pelvic lymph node" are two lymph nodes, each of which is approximately 0.5 cm greatest dimension, surrounded by adipose tissue. The nodes are submitted entirely for frozen section.

FROZEN SECTION DIAGNOSIS (one block): Two lymph nodes free of tumor. MRV/elm

6. In formalin labeled "prostate gland" is a 33 gram radical prostatectomy consisting of a 26 gram, 4.5 x 3.5 x 3.2 cm prostate gland and bilateral seminal vesicles, 3.0 x 1.8 x 1.2 cm on the right and 2.8 x 2.0 x 0.8 cm on the left. The surface of the specimen is unremarkable. The entire specimen is covered with India and further marked as follows: yellow - posterior, green - apex, red - anterior, blue - bladder neck. The cut surface of the gland is gray-white and brown concretions are noted in the right lobe. Discrete tumor cannot be grossly recognized. The seminal vesicles are unremarkable. The prostate gland is sectioned into ten sagittal slices (A-J) and totally submitted in 20 blocks: left side - A through E, and right side - F through J. Slices A and J are transversely sectioned for submission; B-I are submitted as sagittal sections. Samples of left and right seminal vesicle bases are submitted in blocks 21 and 22, respectively. JH/elm

MICRO:
1, 2, 3, 4, and 5. Microscopic examined.

6. The tumor is present in an approximately 1.0 cm greatest dimension area of the left side of the posterior aspect of the gland. The tumor is markedly atrophic, presumably secondary to hormonal therapy. The extent of the atrophy is such that the tumor is almost

Document#: 457952 THIS COPY FOR: Robert Badalament, M.D.

CRITTENTON HOSPITAL
SURGICAL PATHOLOGY REPORT

NAME OF PATIENT	PATIENT NO.	SURGPATH ACCESSION	DATE
Marsee, Bruce	218739013	899-7780	07/06/99

indistinguishable from the surrounding tissue. The Gleason's grade is difficult to assess, due to the extreme atrophy, but is judged to be 3 + 3. No apparent extension to extraprostatic tissue or inked edges of the specimen is seen. No apparent vascular invasion is seen. The tumor is estimated to involve less than 5% of the total volume of the gland.

/slm
7/8/99

SNOP 8143

Special stains: No

Electronically Signed

cc: Robert Badalament, M.D.

 THIS COPY FOR: Robert Badalament, M.D.

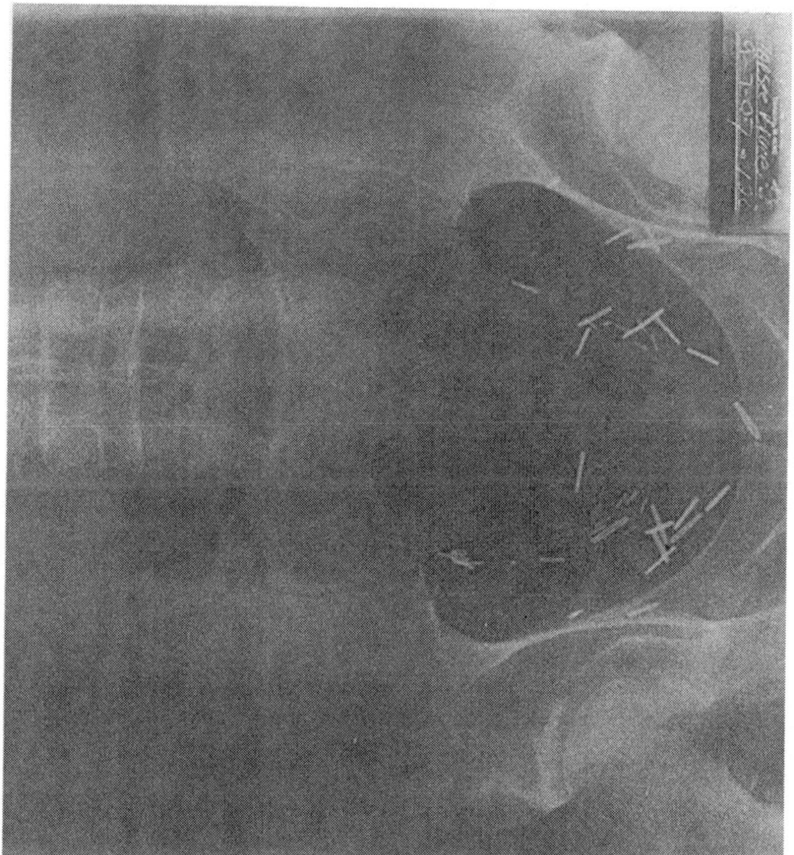

ABOUT THE AUTHOR

Bruce Edward Marsee grew up in the foothills of Southeastern Kentucky when seventy-five percent of all high school graduates went north to find work. After a stint of broadcasting at a local radio station Bruce became a restless eighteen-year-old and hitched up for a two year stint with the United States Marines. In 1996 Bruce took early retirement from successful careers in Information Technology and Business Intelligence. Bruce and wife Sharon now spend time between their homes in Michigan where they enjoy their three children, two granddaughters, porch sitting and traveling.

Published Works:

The Art of Porch Sitting

Other Published works by the author include features for:

Aviation History Magazine

Lands End Catalogue

Life Steps Monthly

Lincoln & Mercury **FRONTLINE** Magazine

Local and Major Newspapers

Prostate Cancer *appeared as a series of articles in the Fenton, Michigan Tri-County Times during 1999. They have been updated and edited for book form.*

Bruce Edward Marsee *grew up in the foothills of Southeastern Kentucky when seventy-five percent of all high school graduates went north to find work. After a stint at broadcasting Bruce became a restless eighteen-year-old and hitched up for a two year stint with the United States Marines. 1996 Bruce took early retirement from successful careers in Information Technology and Business Intelligence. Bruce and wife Sharon now spend time between their homes in Michigan where they enjoy their three children, two Grandchildren, porch sitting and traveling.*

Robert A. Badalament, M.D. FACS. was born and raised in the Detroit area. After graduating from Cranbrook High School, he obtained his B.S. in biology at Southern Methodist University and M.D. at Emory University School of Medicine. He completed his urologic residency at Henry Ford Hospital followed by a two-year urologic-oncology fellowship at Memorial Sloan-Kettering Center. In 1987, he began working at the Ohio State University Medical Center and later went on to become Chief of the Division of Urology, Director of the Urologic Residency Training Program, and Director of Urologic-Oncology at the Arthur G. James Comprehensive Cancer Center.

Dr. Badalament is certified by the American Board of Urology and is a Fellow of the American College of Surgeons. He has written or co-authored over 100 publications.

"Use his book as a guide to help you make the best choices for yourself."

Robert Badalament, MD. FACS.

Would you like to see your manuscript become a book?

If you are interested in becoming a PublishAmerica author, please submit your manuscript for possible publication to us at:

acquisitions@publishamerica.com

You may also mail in your manuscript to:

PublishAmerica
PO Box 151
Frederick, MD 21705

We also offer free graphics for Children's Picture Books!

---

www.publishamerica.com

PublishAmerica

CPSIA information can be obtained at www.ICGtesting.com
Printed in the USA
BVOW081306280413
319242BV00001B/18/P

9 781627 096935